Grammar +Plus Writing

START

2

DARAKWON

저자 약력

전지원

미국 오리건 주립대 Linguistics 석사
(현) 한국 외국어대학교 외국어연수 평가원 영어 전임강사
〈내공 중학 영작문〉(다락원), 〈Grammar Mate〉(다락원),
〈Grammar's Cool〉(YBM), 〈빠르게 잡는 영문법〉(천재교육) 등 다수의 교재 공저

박혜영

미국 하와이 주립대 Second Language Studies 석사
(현) 한국 외국어대학교 외국어연수 평가원 영어 전임강사
〈내공 중학 영작문〉(다락원), 〈Grammar Mate〉(다락원),
〈Grammar's Cool〉(YBM), 〈빠르게 잡는 영문법〉(천재교육) 등 다수의 교재 공저

Grammar Plus Writing START 2

지은이 전지원, 박혜영
펴낸이 정규도
펴낸곳 (주)다락원

개정판 1쇄 발행 2023년 12월 11일
개정판 2쇄 발행 2024년 2월 26일

편집 정연순, 홍인표, 서정아
디자인 김민지, 포레스트
영문 감수 Michael A. Putlack

다락원 경기도 파주시 문발로 211
내용문의 (02) 736-2031 내선 501, 503
구입문의 (02) 736-2031 내선 250~252
Fax (02) 732-2037
출판등록 1977년 9월 16일 제406-2008-000007호

ISBN 978-89-277-8069-4 64740
     978-89-277-8067-0 64740(set)

http://www.darakwon.co.kr

다락원 홈페이지를 방문하시면 상세한 출판 정보와 함께 동영상 강좌,
MP3 자료 등의 다양한 어학 정보를 얻으실 수 있습니다.

Grammar +Plus Writing

START

2

STRUCTURES 구성과 특징

Grammar Plus Writing START 시리즈는

- 각 문법 사항을 이해하기 쉽게 구성하여 기초 영문법을 쉽고 재미있게 학습할 수 있습니다.
- 학습한 문법 요소를 영작과 연계하여 문법 지식과 영작 능력을 동시에 향상시킬 수 있습니다.
- 학교 내신 및 서술형 문제에 효과적으로 대비할 수 있습니다.

문법 설명

사진과 함께 대표 예문을 확인하고, 표를 통해 핵심 문법 사항을 간략히 정리할 수 있어요.

PRACTICE

문제를 통해 학습한 내용을 이해했는지 바로 체크해볼 수 있어요.

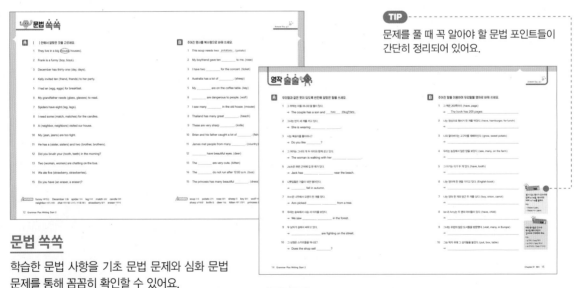

TIP

문제를 풀 때 꼭 알아야 할 문법 포인트들이 간단히 정리되어 있어요.

문법 쏙쏙

학습한 문법 사항을 기초 문법 문제와 심화 문법 문제를 통해 꼼꼼히 확인할 수 있어요.

영작 술술

학습한 문법 사항을 영작과 연계하여 연습할 수 있어요. 영작 술술 A는 본격적인 영작에 들어가기 전 준비 과정으로 활용할 수 있으며, B에서는 완전한 영어 문장을 써 볼 수 있어요.

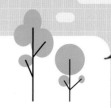

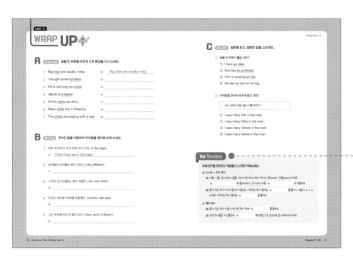

WRAP UP

각 Unit에서 배운 내용을 문법·영작·내신 문제를
통해 다시 한번 정리할 수 있어요.

개념 REVIEW

꼭 기억해야 할 중요 문법 개념들을 빈칸 채우기를
통해 복습할 수 있어요.

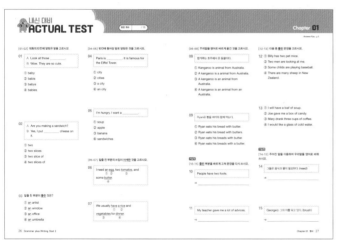

내신 대비 ACTUAL TEST

챕터가 끝날 때마다 배운 내용을 종합적으로 확인
해 볼 수 있어요. 다양한 내신 유형과 서술형 문제에
대비할 수 있으며, 자신의 실력을 평가할 수 있어요.

WORKBOOK

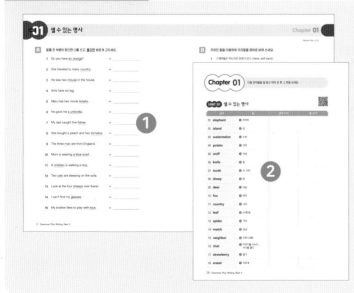

① Grammar & Writing Practice

본책에서 학습한 내용을 A에서는 문법 문제,
B에서는 영작 문제를 통해 복습할 수 있어요.

② Word Practice

본문에서 쓰인 필수 어휘를 듣고 따라 쓰며, 영작
에 유용한 단어들을 복습하고 정리할 수 있어요.

📖 온라인 부가자료 | www.darakwon.co.kr

다락원 홈페이지에서 무료로 부가자료를 다운로드
하거나 웹에서 이용할 수 있습니다.

CONTENTS 목차

Chapter

01

명사

학습목표

1　명사의 의미를 알아보고, 단수 명사와 복수 명사의 형태와 쓰임을 알아봐요.

2　셀 수 없는 명사의 종류를 알아보고, 셀 수 없는 명사의 수량 표현을 익혀요.

UNIT 01 셀 수 있는 명사

1 a/an + 단수 명사

She is eating **a** sandwich.

He is eating **an** apple.

a + 자음		an + 모음	
a book	책 한 권	**an** artist	화가 한 명
a dog	개 한 마리	**an** elephant	코끼리 한 마리
a friend	친구 한 명	**an** island	섬 한 개
a house	집 한 채	**an** orange	오렌지 한 개
a tree	나무 한 그루	**an** umbrella	우산 한 개

☑ 사람, 사물, 장소 등의 이름을 가리켜 **명사**라고 해요. 명사는 책(book), 연필(pencil)처럼 **셀 수 있는 명사**와 물(water), 공기(air)처럼 **셀 수 없는 명사**로 구별해요.

☑ 셀 수 있는 명사가 하나일 때 **자음**으로 시작하는 명사 앞에는 **a**를 붙이고, **모음(a, e, i, o, u)**으로 시작하는 명사 앞에는 **an**을 붙여요.

PRACTICE 1 a/an 넣기

❶ ____a____ cup
❷ _____ boy
❸ _____ egg
❹ _____ horse

❺ _____ office
❻ _____ desk
❼ _____ watermelon
❽ _____ uncle

2 복수 명사

two orang**es**　　　　six dish**es**　　　　three **fish**　　　　four **children**

명사의 종류	규칙		
대부분의 명사	+-s	apple → apple**s**	boy → boy**s**
-sh, -ch, -s, -x, -o로 끝나는 명사	+-es	dish → dish**es** bus → bus**es** potato → potato**es**	watch → watch**es** box → box**es** tomato → tomato**es**
「자음+y」로 끝나는 명사	y를 i로 고치고+-es	baby → bab**ies**	city → cit**ies**
-f, -fe로 끝나는 명사	-f, -fe를 v로 고치고+-es	wolf → wol**ves**	knife → kni**ves**
불규칙 명사	—	man → **men** child → **children** foot → **feet** fish → **fish** deer → **deer**	woman → **women** mouse → **mice** tooth → **teeth** sheep → **sheep** person → **people**

☑ 셀 수 있는 명사가 **둘 이상**이면 명사 뒤에 **-s / -es**를 붙여요.
☑ 어떤 명사들은 자신들만의 **불규칙한 복수형**을 갖고 있으므로 잘 외워두어야 해요.

PRACTICE 2　명사의 복수형 만들기

❶ a pencil　→ two ___pencils___　　❺ a woman　→ two _____

❷ a fox　→ three _____　　❻ a mouse　→ four _____

❸ a country　→ six _____　　❼ a tooth　→ five _____

❹ a leaf　→ ten _____　　❽ a sheep　→ nine _____

문법 쏙쏙

A ( ) 안에서 알맞은 것을 고르세요.

1   They live in a big (house, houses).

2   Frank is a funny (boy, boys).

3   December has thirty-one (day, days).

4   Kelly invited ten (friend, friends) to her party.

5   I had an (egg, eggs) for breakfast.

6   My grandfather needs (glass, glasses) to read.

7   Spiders have eight (leg, legs).

8   I need some (match, matches) for the candles.

9   A (neighbor, neighbors) visited our house.

10   My (jean, jeans) are too tight.

11   He has a (sister, sisters) and two (brother, brothers).

12   Did you brush your (tooth, teeth) in the morning?

13   Two (woman, women) are chatting on the bus.

14   We ate five (strawberry, strawberries).

15   Do you have (an eraser, a eraser)?

 WORDS   funny 재미있는   December 12월   spider 거미   leg 다리   match 성냥   candle 양초
neighbor 이웃 (사람)   chat 이야기를 나누다, 수다를 떨다   strawberry 딸기   eraser 지우개

B 주어진 명사를 복수형으로 바꿔 쓰세요.

1 This soup needs two ___potatoes___ . (potato)

2 My boyfriend gave ten _____ to me. (rose)

3 I have two _____ for the concert. (ticket)

4 Australia has a lot of _____ . (sheep)

5 My _____ are on the coffee table. (key)

6 _____ are dangerous to people. (wolf)

7 I saw many _____ in the old house. (mouse)

8 Thailand has many great _____ . (beach)

9 These are very sharp _____ . (knife)

10 Brian and his father caught a lot of _____ . (fish)

11 James met people from many _____ . (country)

12 _____ have beautiful eyes. (deer)

13 The _____ are very cute. (kitten)

14 The _____ do not run after 12:00 a.m. (bus)

15 The princess has many beautiful _____ . (dress)

 WORDS soup 수프 potato 감자 rose 장미 sheep 양 key 열쇠 wolf 늑대 dangerous 위험한
sharp 날카로운 knife 칼 deer 사슴 kitten 새끼 고양이 princess 공주

A 우리말과 같은 뜻이 되도록 빈칸에 알맞은 말을 쓰세요.

1 그 부부는 아들 하나와 딸 둘이 있다.

→ The couple has a son and ___two___ ___daughters___ .

2 그녀는 반지 세 개를 끼고 있다.

→ She is wearing _____ _____ .

3 너는 복숭아를 좋아하니?

→ Do you like _____?

4 그 여자는 그녀의 개 두 마리와 함께 걷고 있다.

→ The woman is walking with her _____ _____ .

5 Jack은 해변 근처에 집 한 채가 있다.

→ Jack has _____ _____ near the beach.

6 나뭇잎들은 가을이 되면 떨어진다.

→ _____ fall in autumn.

7 Ann은 나무에서 오렌지 한 개를 땄다.

→ Ann picked _____ _____ from a tree.

8 우리는 숲속에서 사슴 세 마리를 보았다.

→ We saw _____ _____ in the forest.

9 두 남자가 길에서 싸우고 있다.

→ _____ _____ are fighting on the street.

10 그 상점은 스카프들을 파나요?

→ Does the shop sell _____?

B 주어진 말을 이용하여 우리말을 영어로 바꿔 쓰세요.

1 그 책은 200쪽이다. (have, page)

→ _____ The book has 200 pages. _____

2 나는 점심으로 햄버거 한 개를 먹었다. (have, hamburger, for lunch)

→ _____

3 나의 할아버지는 고구마를 재배하신다. (grow, sweet potato)

→ _____

4 우리는 농장에서 많은 양을 보았다. (see, many, on the farm)

→ _____

5 그 아기는 이가 두 개 있다. (have, tooth)

→ _____

6 나는 영어책 한 권을 가지고 있다. (English book)

→ _____

TIP 1

셀 수 있는 명사가 단수이면 앞에 a/an을, 복수이면 뒤에 -s/-es를 붙여요.

e.g.
- I have a pen.
- I have two pens.

7 나는 양파 한 개와 당근 두 개를 샀다. (buy, onion, carrot)

→ _____

8 Ian과 Amy는 두 명의 아이들이 있다. (have, child)

→ _____

TIP 2

어떤 명사들은 단수와 복수일 때의 모양이 같으므로 주의해야 해요.

e.g.
- a fish / two fish
- a deer / two deer
- a sheep / two sheep

9 그녀는 유럽의 많은 도시들을 방문했다. (visit, many, in Europe)

→ _____

10 그는 탁자 위에 그 상자들을 놓았다. (put, box, table)

→ _____

WRAP UP

A Grammar 밑줄 친 부분을 바르게 고쳐 문장을 다시 쓰세요.

1 Big citys are usually noisy. ➡ Big cities are usually noisy.

2 I bought some tomatos. ➡ _____

3 He is carrying two boxs. ➡ _____

4 Jejudo is a island. ➡ _____

5 All the dishs are dirty. ➡ _____

6 Many wolfs live in America. ➡ _____

7 The childs are playing with a ball. ➡ _____

B Writing 주어진 말을 이용하여 우리말을 영어로 바꿔 쓰세요.

1 여우 세 마리가 우리 안에 있다. (fox, in the cage)

➡ Three foxes are in the cage.

2 남자들과 여자들은 매우 다르다. (very different)

➡ _____

3 그녀의 이(치아들)는 매우 하얗다. (her, very white)

➡ _____

4 우리는 작년에 5개국을 방문했다. (country, last year)

➡ _____

5 그는 부산에 숙모 한 분이 있다. (have, aunt, in Busan)

➡ _____

C 　내신 대비　질문을 읽고, 알맞은 답을 고르세요.

1 밑줄 친 부분이 틀린 것은?

① I have an idea.

② She has an umbrella.

③ Tom is wearing an hat.

④ He saw an ant on his leg.

2 우리말을 영어로 바르게 옮긴 것은?

> 나는 강에서 많은 물고기를 보았다.

① I saw many fish in the river.

② I saw many fishs in the river.

③ I saw many fishies in the river.

④ I saw many fishes in the river.

개념 Review

아래 빈칸을 채우면서 개념을 다시 한번 익혀보세요.

① a / an + 단수 명사

- ☑ 사람, 사물, 장소 등의 이름을 가리켜 명사라고 해요. 명사는 책(book), 연필(pencil)처럼 **①** ＿＿＿＿＿＿＿＿＿ 와 물(water), 공기(air)처럼 **②** ＿＿＿＿＿＿＿＿＿ 로 구별해요.

- ☑ 셀 수 있는 명사가 하나일 때 자음으로 시작하는 명사 앞에는 **③** ＿＿＿＿＿＿ 를 붙이고, 모음(a, e, i, o, u)으로 시작하는 명사 앞에는 **④** ＿＿＿＿＿＿ 을 붙여요.

② 복수 명사

- ☑ 셀 수 있는 명사가 둘 이상이면 명사 뒤에 **⑤** ＿＿＿＿＿＿ 를 붙여요.

- ☑ 어떤 명사들은 자신들만의 **⑥** ＿＿＿＿＿＿ 복수형을 갖고 있으므로 잘 외워두어야 해요.

UNIT 02 셀 수 없는 명사

1 셀 수 없는 명사

Julie lives in **Canada**.

I love **music**.

셀 수 없는 명사	
고유 명사 (이름, 지명, 국가, 언어, 요일 등)	Minho, Seoul, Canada, English, Sunday
추상 명사 (눈에 보이지 않는 것)	love, peace, luck, beauty, music, work, time
물질 명사 (일정한 모양과 크기가 없는 것)	• water, juice, coffee, tea, milk, soup, oil • bread, butter, cheese, meat, soap • salt, sugar, pepper, rice
전체를 나타내는 명사	furniture 가구(류) fruit 과일(류) mail 우편(물) money 돈

☑ **셀 수 없는 명사**는 a / an을 붙이거나 복수형을 만들 수 없고, 항상 **단수**로 사용해요.
  e.g. I like *a milk / milks*. (X)   I like *milk*. (O)

PRACTICE 1 알맞은 말 고르기

❶ (A sugar, Sugar) is sweet.

❷ The baker is making (a bread, bread).

❸ She drinks (coffee, coffees) every day.

❹ I have some (money, moneys) in my pocket.

2 셀 수 없는 명사의 수량 표현

a piece of cake

two glasses of milk

a loaf of bread

four bars of soap

수량 표현	명사	수량 표현	명사
a piece of 한 조각[점/마디]의	bread, cheese, cake, furniture, advice	**a slice of** (얇게 썬) 한 장의	bread, cheese
a cup of 한 컵[잔]의	coffee, tea, water	**a loaf of** 한 덩어리의	bread
a glass[bottle] of 한 잔[병]의	water, juice, milk	**a box of** 한 상자의	candy
a bowl of 한 그릇의	rice, soup	**a bar of** (막대 모양) 한 개의	soap, chocolate

☑ 셀 수 없는 명사는 **모양**이나 **담는 그릇을 단위**로 해서 수량을 표현해요.

☑ 셀 수 없는 명사의 복수형은 단위 명사를 복수로 써줘요. **e.g.** a cup of tea, two cups of tea

PRACTICE 2 알맞은 수량 표현 넣기

❶ I bought a _____loaf_____ of bread.

❷ He ordered two _____ of coffee.

❸ A _____ of candy is a good gift.

❹ Jack quickly finished a _____ of rice.

문법 쏙쏙

A 밑줄 친 명사가 해당하는 것에 V표 하세요.

		셀 수 있는 명사	셀 수 없는 명사
1	Do you have enough <u>money</u>?	☐	☑
2	She is listening to <u>music</u>.	☐	☐
3	My boyfriend sang a <u>song</u> for me.	☐	☐
4	They did a lot of <u>work</u> today.	☐	☐
5	Mike gave me some <u>chocolate</u>.	☐	☐
6	Mr. Simpson has two <u>sons</u>.	☐	☐
7	<u>London</u> is an interesting city.	☐	☐
8	Plants need <u>water</u>.	☐	☐
9	Leo wrote many <u>letters</u> to Jane.	☐	☐
10	I didn't get any <u>mail</u>.	☐	☐
11	He is drinking some <u>orange juice</u>.	☐	☐
12	I had no <u>luck</u> on my exam.	☐	☐
13	He bought an expensive <u>chair</u>.	☐	☐
14	Our bodies need <u>salt</u>.	☐	☐
15	Sophie loves <u>animals</u>.	☐	☐

WORDS interesting 흥미로운   luck 운, 행운   body 몸, 신체   salt 소금   animal 동물

B ( ) 안에서 알맞은 수량 표현을 고르세요.

1 I usually have (a slice of, ~~a cup of~~) tea in the morning.

2 We bought (a bowl of, a loaf of) bread.

3 He gave me (a glass of, a piece of) cheese.

4 (A bar of, A bottle of) lemonade is 10 dollars.

5 I put (a slice of, a loaf of) cheese on my sandwich.

6 I'm not hungry. I'll just have (a piece of, a glass of) juice.

7 They ordered (three bowls of, three bars of) onion soup.

8 I ate (a slice of, a bar of) chocolate.

9 He brought me (a cup of, a bar of) coffee.

10 The boy drank (a piece of, a glass of) milk.

11 My mom baked (four loaves of, four cups of) bread.

12 Emily gave me (a loaf of, a box of) candy for my birthday.

13 We use (two loaves of, two bars of) soap every month.

14 (A bowl of, A piece of) rice is not enough for Sean.

15 Amy ate (a bars of, a piece of) cake for dessert.

WORDS lemonade 레모네이드 **put** 놓다, 두다 **order** 주문하다 **bake** 굽다 **soap** 비누 **dessert** 디저트, 후식

영작 술술

A 우리말과 같은 뜻이 되도록 빈칸에 알맞은 말을 쓰세요.

1 우리는 시간이 많지 않다.

→ We don't have much ____time____ .

2 사랑은 모두에게 중요하다.

→ _____ is important to everyone.

3 Justin은 록 음악을 좋아한다.

→ Justin likes rock _____.

4 Brian은 할 일이 너무 많다.

→ Brian has too much _____ to do.

5 충고 감사해요.

→ Thank you for your _____.

6 나는 빵에 약간의 버터를 발랐다.

→ I put some _____ on my bread.

7 Jim은 밥 한 공기를 김치와 먹었다.

→ Jim had _____ _____ _____ rice with kimchi.

8 너는 샌드위치를 위해 빵 두 장이 필요하다.

→ You need _____ _____ _____ bread for a sandwich.

9 커피 한 잔 주세요.

→ I would like _____ _____ _____ coffee, please.

10 그는 햄버거 한 개와 주스 한 잔을 주문했다.

→ He ordered a hamburger and _____ _____ _____ juice.

B 주어진 말을 이용하여 우리말을 영어로 바꿔 쓰세요.

1 우리는 숙제가 너무 많다. (have, too much)

➡ ___We have too much homework.___

2 Emily는 매일 음악을 듣는다. (listen to, every day)

➡ _____

3 생쥐들은 치즈를 좋아하나요? (mice)

➡ _____

4 돈이 전부는 아니다. (not, everything)

➡ _____

5 7월 1일은 일요일이다. (July 1)

➡ _____

6 그녀는 과일을 많이 먹는다. (eat, a lot of)

➡ _____

7 나는 내 방에 가구가 좀 필요하다. (some, in my room)

➡ _____

8 나는 하루에 물 8잔을 마신다. (drink, glass, a day)

➡ _____

9 Cathy는 비누 두 개를 샀다. (buy, soap)

➡ _____

10 Mark는 하루에 차 두 잔을 즐긴다. (enjoy, cup, a day)

➡ _____

TIP 1

셀 수 없는 명사는 앞에 a/an이나 뒤에 -s/-es 를 붙일 수 없고 항상 단수로만 써야 해요.

e.g.
- I like a music. (×)
- I like musics. (×)
- I like music. (○)

TIP 2

셀 수 없는 명사 앞에 함께 쓸 수 있는 표현들을 알아두세요.

e.g.
- some food 약간의 음식
- a lot of money 많은 돈
- too much work
  너무 많은 일

WRAP UP

A Grammar 밑줄 친 부분을 바르게 고쳐 문장을 다시 쓰세요.

1 Everybody wants <u>peaces</u>. ➡ Everybody wants peace.

2 I drank <u>a slice of</u> water. ➡ _____

3 <u>A Seoul</u> is a big city. ➡ _____

4 I ordered <u>a glass of</u> cream soup. ➡ _____

5 He doesn't have any <u>moneys</u>. ➡ _____

6 I had <u>two cup of coffee</u> today. ➡ _____

7 We ate <u>four bar of chocolates</u>. ➡ _____

B Writing 주어진 말을 이용하여 우리말을 영어로 바꿔 쓰세요.

1 나는 종이 한 장이 필요하다. (a piece of)

➡ I need a piece of paper.

2 당신의 충고는 도움이 되었어요. (be, helpful)

➡ _____

3 그녀는 미국에서 온 우편물이 좀 있어요. (have, some, from America)

➡ _____

4 나는 빵 한 덩어리를 살 거야. (be going to)

➡ _____

5 물과 기름은 섞이지 않는다. (not, mix)

➡ _____

C 내신 대비 질문을 읽고, 알맞은 답을 고르세요.

1 다음 중 문장이 올바른 것은?

① An apple juice is sweet.

② He makes a lot of money.

③ I want a sugar in my coffee.

④ The band played some musics.

2 우리말을 영어로 바르게 옮긴 것은?

> 나는 아침으로 빵 두 조각을 먹었다.

① I had two breads for breakfast.

② I had two piece of bread for breakfast.

③ I had two pieces of bread for breakfast.

④ I had two pieces of breads for breakfast.

개념 Review

아래 빈칸을 채우면서 개념을 다시 한번 익혀보세요.

❶ 셀 수 없는 명사

☑ 셀 수 없는 명사는 a / an을 붙이거나 복수형을 만들 수 없고, 항상 ❶ _____ 로 사용해요.

❷ 셀 수 없는 명사의 수량 표현

☑ 셀 수 없는 명사는 ❷ _____ 이나 ❸ _____ 을 단위로 해서 수량을 표현해요.

☑ 셀 수 없는 명사의 복수형은 ❹ _____ 를 복수로 써줘요.

[01-02] 대화의 빈칸에 알맞은 말을 고르시오.

01

> A Look at those _____.
> B Wow. They are so cute.

① baby
② babis
③ babys
④ babies

02

> A Are you making a sandwich?
> B Yes, I put _____ cheese on it.

① two
② two slices
③ two slice of
④ two slices of

03 밑줄 친 부분이 틀린 것은?

① an artist
② an window
③ an office
④ an umbrella

[04-05] 빈칸에 들어갈 말로 알맞은 것을 고르시오.

04

> Paris is _____. It is famous for the Eiffel Tower.

① city
② cities
③ a city
④ an city

05

> I'm hungry. I want a _____.

① soup
② apple
③ banana
④ sandwiches

[06-07] 밑줄 친 부분의 쓰임이 어색한 것을 고르시오.

06

> I need an egg, two tomatos, and
>   ① ②   ③
> some butter.
>   ④

07

> We usually have a rice and
>   ① ②
> vegetables for dinner.
>   ③   ④

[08-09] 우리말을 영어로 바르게 옮긴 것을 고르시오.

08
캥거루는 호주에서 온 동물이다.

① Kangaroo is animal from Australia.
② A kangaroo is a animal from Australia.
③ A kangaroo is an animal from Australia.
④ A kangaroo is an animal from an Australia.

09
Ryan은 빵을 버터와 함께 먹는다.

① Ryan eats his bread with butter.
② Ryan eats his bread with butters.
③ Ryan eats his breads with butter.
④ Ryan eats his breads with a butter.

서술형
[10-11] 틀린 부분을 바르게 고쳐 문장을 다시 쓰시오.

10
People have two foots.

➜ _____

11
My teacher gave me a lot of advices.

➜ _____

[12-13] 다음 중 틀린 문장을 고르시오.

12 ① Billy has two pet mice.
② Two men are looking at me.
③ Some childs are playing baseball.
④ There are many sheep in New Zealand.

13 ① I will have a loaf of soup.
② Joe gave me a box of candy.
③ Mary drank three cups of coffee.
④ I would like a glass of cold water.

서술형
[14-15] 주어진 말을 이용하여 우리말을 영어로 바꿔 쓰시오.

14
그들은 음식과 물이 필요하다. (need)

➜ _____

15
George는 그의 이를 닦고 있다. (brush)

➜ _____

02

대명사

학습목표

1   인칭대명사의 종류와 쓰임에 대해 알아봐요.

2   지시대명사의 종류와 쓰임에 대해 알아보고, 지시형용사로서의 쓰임도 알아봐요.

UNIT 01 인칭대명사

1 주격 / 목적격

She loves us.

Look at the phone. It is on the desk.

주격 (~은/는)	
I know the movie.	나는 그 영화를 안다.
We love music.	우리는 음악을 좋아한다.
You look happy.	너(희)는 행복해 보인다.
He likes sports.	그는 스포츠를 좋아한다.
She loves fruit.	그녀는 과일을 좋아한다.
It is on the desk.	그것은 책상 위에 있다.
They play soccer.	그들은 축구를 한다.

목적격 (~을/를)	
Amy loves **me**.	Amy는 나를 사랑한다.
He teaches **us**.	그는 우리를 가르친다.
We know **you**.	우리는 너(희)를 안다.
Gary visited **him**.	Gary는 그를 방문했다.
Steve helped **her**.	Steve는 그녀를 도와주었다.
I saw **it** over there.	나는 저기에서 그것을 보았다.
We invited **them**.	우리는 그들을 초대했다.

☑ **인칭대명사**는 '나, 너, 그, 그것'처럼 **사람이나 사물의 이름을 대신해서 쓰는 말**이에요.

☑ 인칭대명사의 **주격**은 '~은/는'을 의미하며, **주어**를 대신해서 사용해요.

☑ 인칭대명사의 **목적격**은 '~을/를'을 의미하며, **목적어**를 대신해서 사용해요.

PRACTICE 1 알맞은 인칭대명사 넣기

❶ 그것은 좋은 영화이다.   ➡   It   is a good movie.

❷ 그들은 Bob을 알지 못한다.   ➡   _____ don't know Bob.

❸ 나는 그녀를 매우 사랑한다.   ➡ I love _____ so much.

❹ 나의 삼촌은 나를 방문했다.   ➡ My uncle visited _____.

2 소유격 / 소유대명사

These are **my** books.

No, they're **mine**.

소유격 (~의)		소유대명사 (~의 것)	
This is **my** hat.	이것은 나의 모자이다.	This pencil is **mine**.	이 연필은 나의 것이다.
We love **our** dog.	우리는 우리의 개를 좋아한다.	The toys are **ours**.	그 장난감들은 우리의 것이다.
Is this **your** car?	이것이 너의(너희) 자동차니?	Is this cat **yours**?	이 고양이는 너의(너희) 것이니?
Sam lost **his** bag.	Sam은 그의 가방을 분실했다.	The shoes are **his**.	그 신발은 그의 것이다.
That is **her** book.	저것은 그녀의 책이다.	The scarf is **hers**.	그 스카프는 그녀의 것이다.
Their house is big.	그들의 집은 크다.	The bikes are **theirs**.	그 자전거들은 그들의 것이다.
The dog ate **its** food.	그 개는 자신의 음식을 먹었다.	—	

☑ 인칭대명사의 **소유격**은 '~의'를 의미하며, 뒤에 **명사**가 따라와요.

☑ **소유대명사**는 「**소유격 + 명사**」를 대신하고 '~의 것'을 의미해요. 소유대명사 뒤에는 명사가 오지 않아요.

  e.g. This book is *mine book*. (X)   This book is *mine*. (O)

PRACTICE 2 알맞은 인칭대명사 넣기

❶ 나는 나의 강아지를 사랑한다. → I love _____my_____ puppy.

❷ 너의 여동생은 똑똑하다. → _____ sister is smart.

❸ 그 지갑은 그녀의 것이다. → The purse is _____.

❹ 그 빨간 차가 너의 것이니? → Is the red car _____?

 문법 쏙쏙

A ( ) 안에서 알맞은 인칭대명사를 고르세요.

1 (They, Their) are good friends.

2 (You, Your) watch looks nice.

3 Paul bought some flowers for (she, her).

4 (It, Its) is a big problem.

5 Jessica is (my, mine) best friend.

6 John always helps (I, me) with my homework.

7 (They, Their) house is at the end of the street.

8 Susan lives with (she, her) grandparents.

9 My room is small, but (you, yours) is big.

10 My uncle has a dog. (It, Its) name is Ben.

11 This new computer is (him, his).

12 Tom and (I, me) played badminton yesterday.

13 My hands are clean. I just washed (they, them).

14 He is a famous singer. Everyone knows (him, his).

15 They showed (us, our) a famous place.

 WORDS watch 손목시계 flower 꽃 problem 문제 street 거리, 도로 play badminton 배드민턴을 치다
famous 유명한 everyone 모든 사람, 모두

B 주어진 대명사를 빈칸에 알맞은 형태로 고쳐 쓰세요.

1 Fred has a cat. _____It_____ has black fur. (it)

2 Look at _____! He is singing. (he)

3 Our car is red, but _____ is black. (they)

4 I bought a blue dress. I like _____ so much. (it)

5 I saw Lisa and _____ husband this morning. (she)

6 We spent _____ vacation in Florida. (we)

7 The dog hurt _____ leg. (it)

8 Ann is from America. _____ has blue eyes. (she)

9 I know Mr. Taylor, but I don't know _____ wife. (he)

10 Don't ask _____. I don't know. (I)

11 Jack and Peter are playing with _____ friends. (they)

12 That isn't our bag. _____ is yellow. (we)

13 I hate snakes. _____ are scary. (they)

14 I brush _____ teeth after meals. (I)

15 I am looking for Sarah. Did you see _____? (she)

 WORDS   fur (동물의) 털, 모피   black 검정색; 검은   husband 남편   spend (돈을) 쓰다; (시간을) 보내다   vacation 휴가
hurt 다치게 하다   wife 아내   ask 묻다   yellow 노란색; 노란색의   hate 싫어하다   snake 뱀
scary 무서운   after a meal 식후에

A 우리말과 같은 뜻이 되도록 빈칸에 알맞은 말을 쓰세요.

1 그 어린 소년은 내 남동생이다.

→ The little boy is ___my___ brother.

2 오늘은 너의 생일이다.

→ Today is _____ birthday.

3 우리는 그들을 잘 모른다.

→ We don't know _____ very well.

4 Peter는 항상 나를 도와준다.

→ Peter always helps _____.

5 그녀의 부모님은 너그럽다.

→ _____ parents are generous.

6 그 우산은 그녀의 것이다.

→ The umbrella is _____.

7 나뭇잎 하나가 그것의 나무에서 떨어졌다.

→ A leaf fell from _____ tree.

8 그 돈은 내 것이다.

→ The money is _____.

9 그 개는 우리를 보고 짖었다.

→ The dog barked at _____.

10 그는 그의 신발을 찾았나요?

→ Did he find _____ shoes?

B 주어진 말을 이용하여 우리말을 영어로 바꿔 쓰세요.

1 Sally는 내 여동생이 아니다. (sister)

➡ Sally is not my sister.

2 그녀의 성은 Kim이다. (last name)

➡

3 그 책들은 네 것이니? (the books)

➡

4 너는 그녀를 알고 있니? (know)

➡

5 그 가방은 그의 것이 아니다. (the bag)

➡

6 그 아기는 그에게 미소 지었다. (smile at)

➡

7 그 아이들은 그들의 음식을 먹었다. (children, eat, food)

➡

8 John은 나에게 매일 전화한다. (call, every day)

➡

9 Jack은 그의 할머니를 사랑한다. (grandmother)

➡

10 Diana는 우리를 그 파티에 초대했다. (invite, to, party)

➡

TIP 1

인칭대명사는 그 역할에 따라 주격, 목적격, 소유격, 소유대명사로 쓰여요.

e.g.
- I know Tom. (나는)
- Tom knows me. (나를)
- My bag is blue. (나의)
- The bag is mine. (나의 것)

TIP 2

소유대명사는 「소유격+명사」를 대신하고 '~의 것'을 의미해요.

e.g.
- This is my pen.
- This pen is mine. (mine = my + pen)

WRAP UP

A Grammar 밑줄 친 부분을 바르게 고쳐 문장을 다시 쓰세요.

1 <u>His</u> lives in New York. → He lives in New York.

2 <u>Theirs</u> dog is white. → _____

3 The jacket is <u>her</u>. → _____

4 Do you know <u>they</u>? → _____

5 We saw Jane and <u>she</u> boyfriend. → _____

6 His eyes are blue. <u>My</u> are brown. → _____

7 Do you like <u>us</u> new furniture? → _____

B Writing 주어진 말을 이용하여 우리말을 영어로 바꿔 쓰세요.

1 그들은 나의 사촌들이다. (cousin)

→ They are my cousins.

2 그 사전은 우리의 것이다. (the dictionary)

→ _____

3 Ted는 그의 차를 세차할 것이다. (be going to, wash)

→ _____

4 나의 부모님은 나를 아주 많이 사랑하신다. (parents, so much)

→ _____

5 Mary와 나는 그것의 냄새를 좋아하지 않는다. (smell)

→ _____

C 내신 대비 질문을 읽고, 알맞은 답을 고르세요.

1 다음 중 문장이 올바른 것은?

① The house is theirs.

② Hers name is Anna.

③ No, its not my pen.

④ I will meet he tomorrow.

2 빈칸에 들어갈 말이 순서대로 바르게 짝지어진 것은?

> _____ neighbors are Mr. and Mrs. Smith.
>
> _____ are very nice.

① We – They

② Our – They

③ Our – Their

④ Ours – Theirs

개념 Review

아래 빈칸을 채우면서 개념을 다시 한번 익혀보세요.

❶ 인칭대명사 (주격 / 목적격)

☑ ❶ _____ 는 '나, 너, 그, 그것'처럼 사람이나 사물의 이름을 대신해서 쓰는 말이에요.

☑ 인칭대명사의 주격은 '~은 / 는'을 의미하며, ❷ _____ 를 대신해서 사용해요.

☑ 인칭대명사의 목적격은 '~을 / 를'을 의미하며, ❸ _____ 를 대신해서 사용해요.

❷ 인칭대명사 (소유격 / 소유대명사)

☑ 인칭대명사의 소유격은 '~의'를 의미하며, 뒤에 ❹ _____ 가 따라와요.

☑ 소유대명사는 「❺ _____ 」를 대신하고 '~의 것'을 의미해요. 소유대명사 뒤에는 명사가 오지 않아요.

UNIT 02 지시대명사

1 This / That

This is my new dress.

That is the bridge.

This		That	
This is my bag.	이것은 내 가방이다.	**That** is a nice house.	저것은 멋진 집이다.
This is my friend Joy.	이 사람은 내 친구 Joy야.	**That** is my teacher.	저분은 내 선생님이야.
Is **this** your camera?	이것은 네 카메라니?	Is **that** your umbrella?	저것은 네 우산이니?
This hotel is expensive.	이 호텔은 비싸다.	**That man** is Mr. Chen.	저 남자는 Chen 씨이다.

☑ 지시대명사 **this**는 **가까이 있는 대상**을, **that**은 **멀리 있는 대상**을 가리킬 때 써요. this와 that은 모두 **하나의 대상**을 가리킬 때만 사용해요.

☑ this와 that은 뒤에 명사를 꾸며 주는 **지시형용사**로도 쓰일 수 있어요.

    e.g. this *book*　**that** *girl*

PRACTICE 1　**this / that 넣기**

❶ 이것은 너의 펜이니? → Is ＿＿＿this＿＿＿ your pen?

❷ 저 사람은 내 여동생이 아니다. → ＿＿＿＿＿＿ is not my sister.

❸ 이 케이크는 맛있다. → ＿＿＿＿＿＿ cake tastes delicious.

❹ 제게 저 책을 주세요. → Give me ＿＿＿＿＿＿ book, please.

2 These / Those

These are my toys.

Those are monkeys.

These	Those
These are my pens. 이것들은 내 펜이다. **These** are my friends. 이 사람들은 내 친구이다. Are **these** your books? 이것들은 네 책이니? **These houses** are old. 이 집들은 오래되었다.	**Those** are her notebooks. 저것들은 그녀의 공책이다. **Those** are my parents. 저분들은 내 부모님이다. Are **those** your gloves? 저것들은 네 장갑이니? Look at **those stars**! 저 별들을 봐!

☑ **둘 이상의 대상**을 가리킬 때는 this 대신 **these**를, that 대신 **those**를 사용해요.

☑ these와 those가 지시형용사로 쓰일 때는 뒤에 **복수 명사**가 와요.

  e.g. these *boy* (X) these *boys* (O)

PRACTICE 2 **these / those 넣기**

① 저것들은 그의 안경이다. → _____Those_____ are his glasses.

② 이것들은 네 벙어리 장갑이니? → Are _____ your mittens?

③ 이 인형들은 매우 귀엽다. → _____ dolls are very cute.

④ 너는 저 책들을 좋아하니? → Do you like _____ books?

문법 쏙쏙

A ( ) 안에서 알맞은 것을 고르세요.

1 ((This), These) is my pencil.

2 (That, Those) is a nice necklace.

3 Are (this, these) your sneakers?

4 (That, Those) ring is gold.

5 (That, Those) towels are clean.

6 Is (this, these) suit expensive?

7 Do you like (this, these) flowers?

8 (That, Those) are his children.

9 (That, Those) rainbow is beautiful.

10 (This, These) questions are difficult.

11 Pass me (that, those) magazine, please.

12 (This, These) is my cousin Bob.

13 (This, These) vegetables look fresh.

14 Look at (that, those) men over there.

15 I don't understand (this, these) word.

 WORDS necklace 목걸이 sneakers 운동화 ring 반지 towel 수건 suit 정장 rainbow 무지개
question 문제, 질문 difficult 어려운 pass 건네주다 magazine 잡지 cousin 사촌 vegetable 채소
look ~하게 보이다 fresh 신선한 over there 저쪽에 word 단어; 말

B this는 these로, that은 those로 바꿔 문장을 다시 쓰세요.

1 This is a new bike.

→ _These are new bikes._

2 That is my cat.

→ _____

3 This desk is mine.

→ _____

4 That letter is for Peter.

→ _____

5 Is this your umbrella?

→ _____

6 Is that your book?

→ _____

7 I like this picture.

→ _____

8 Look at that cloud.

→ _____

9 Pass me that pencil.

→ _____

10 This is a fun game.

→ _____

WORDS   letter 편지   picture 그림, 사진   cloud 구름   fun 재미있는, 즐거운; 재미

A 우리말과 같은 뜻이 되도록 빈칸에 알맞은 말을 쓰세요.

1 이것은 오늘의 신문이다.

→ _____This_____ _____is_____ today's newspaper.

2 이것은 Paul의 부츠이다.

→ _____ _____ Paul's boots.

3 저분이 네 담임 선생님이니?

→ _____ _____ your homeroom teacher?

4 저것은 Amy의 안경이다.

→ _____ _____ Amy's glasses.

5 당신이 이 노래를 썼나요?

→ Did you write _____ _____?

6 저 수건들은 젖었나요?

→ Are _____ _____ wet?

7 아니오, 이것들은 제 것이 아니에요.

→ No, _____ _____ not mine.

8 저 꽃을 봐. 그것은 아름다워.

→ Look at _____ _____. It is beautiful.

9 저 사람들은 노래를 못 부른다.

→ _____ _____ sing badly.

10 우리는 이 사전이 필요 없다.

→ We don't need _____ _____.

B 주어진 말을 이용하여 우리말을 영어로 바꿔 쓰세요.

1 이것은 내가 좋아하는 향수이다. (perfume)

➡ This is my favorite perfume.

2 저것은 우체국이다. (the post office)

➡

3 이 사람은 내 여동생 Jessica야. (sister)

➡

4 이 담요들은 따뜻하다. (blanket, warm)

➡

5 저 신발은 비싸다. (shoes, expensive)

➡

6 저 사람들은 유명한 배우니? (famous actor)

➡

7 이 스웨터는 당신의 것인가요? (sweater)

➡

8 이것들은 빈 상자인가요? (empty box)

➡

9 이 수프는 맛있다. (soup, delicious)

➡

10 저 학생은 글을 잘 쓴다. (write well)

➡

TIP 1

this/that은 단수 명사, 단수 동사와 함께 쓰고, these/those는 복수 명사, 복수 동사와 함께 써요.

e.g.
- This is an apple.
  These are apples.
- Look at that house.
  Look at those houses.

TIP 2

셀 수 없는 명사는 단수 취급, 짝을 이루는 명사는 복수 취급해요.

e.g.
- this/that milk
- these/those pants
  [shoes, glasses, socks, gloves...]

WRAP UP

A Grammar ( ) 안에서 알맞은 것을 고르세요.

1 (This, These) are not my clothes.

2 (That, Those) are beautiful earrings.

3 Is (that, those) your father?

4 Do you like (this, these) jeans?

5 (That, Those) cat looks sad.

6 (This, These) soap smells good.

7 Did you open (that, those) windows?

B Writing 주어진 말을 이용하여 우리말을 영어로 바꿔 쓰세요.

1 이것은 나의 필통이다. (pencil case)

　➡　This is my pencil case.

2 저 티켓은 무료이다. (ticket, free)

　➡　

3 이것이 당신의 코트인가요? (coat)

　➡　

4 저것들은 그의 양말이다. (socks)

　➡　

5 이 쿠키들은 맛있다. (cookie, delicious)

　➡

C 내신 대비 질문을 읽고, 알맞은 답을 고르세요.

1 밑줄 친 부분이 틀린 것은?

① <u>This</u> milk tastes sour.

② <u>These</u> are my sneakers.

③ Look at <u>that</u> butterfly.

④ Did you draw <u>those</u> picture?

2 우리말을 영어로 바르게 옮긴 것은?

> 나는 너를 위해 이 장미들을 샀다.

① I bought this rose for you.

② I bought this roses for you.

③ I bought these rose for you.

④ I bought these roses for you.

개념 Review

아래 빈칸을 채우면서 개념을 다시 한번 익혀보세요.

❶ **This / That**

☑ 지시대명사 ❶ _____ 는 가까이 있는 대상을, ❷ _____ 은 멀리 있는 대상을 가리킬 때

써요. this와 that은 모두 하나의 대상을 가리킬 때만 사용해요.

☑ this와 that은 뒤에 명사를 꾸며 주는 ❸ _____ 로도 쓰일 수 있어요.

❷ **These / Those**

☑ 둘 이상의 대상을 가리킬 때는 this 대신 ❹ _____ 를, that 대신 ❺ _____ 를 사용해요.

☑ these와 those가 지시형용사로 쓰일 때는 뒤에 ❻ _____ 가 와요.

[01-02] 대화의 빈칸에 알맞은 말을 고르시오.

01

| A | Do you like summer? |
| B | Of course. _____ my favorite season. |

① Its
② It is
③ He is
④ They are

02

| A | Are these your keys? |
| B | Yes, they are _____. |

① I
② my
③ me
④ mine

03 빈칸에 들어갈 말로 알맞지 <u>않은</u> 것은?

I like these _____.

① tea
② songs
③ shoes
④ flowers

[04-05] 빈칸에 들어갈 말로 알맞은 것을 고르시오.

04

Mrs. Johnson has three children.
_____ all smart.

① He is
② She is
③ We are
④ They are

05

David is wearing a hat. _____
color is green.

① It
② Its
③ His
④ Their

서술형
06 다음 문장을 아래와 같이 바꿀 때 빈칸에 알맞은 말을 쓰시오.

Those windows are open.

➡ _____ _____ is open.

07 밑줄 친 부분의 쓰임이 <u>어색한</u> 것은?

These are my photos. I took they at
　①　　　②　　　　③　　　④
the zoo.

Chapter 02

Answer Key p.7

[08-09] 우리말을 영어로 바르게 옮긴 것을 고르시오.

08

> 이곳은 내 자리야. 네 자리가 아니야.

① This is my seat. It is not your.

② This is me seat. It is not your.

③ This is my seat. It is not yours.

④ This is mine seat. It is not yours.

09

> 저 산들은 매우 높다.

① That mountain is very high.

② Those mountain is very high.

③ That mountains are very high.

④ Those mountains are very high.

서술형

[10-11] 틀린 부분을 바르게 고쳐 문장을 다시 쓰시오.

10

> I like Italy. They are a beautiful country.

➡ _____

11

> These are not my slippers. They are her.

➡ _____

[12-13] 다음 중 문장이 올바른 것을 고르시오.

12 ① Ours car is black.

② The dog followed I.

③ This notebook is his.

④ He garden is beautiful.

13 ① This is tall trees.

② That earrings are pretty.

③ Are these your raincoat?

④ Those children are noisy.

서술형

[14-15] 주어진 말을 이용하여 우리말을 영어로 바꿔 쓰시오.

14

> 이 컴퓨터는 우리의 것이다. (computer)

➡ _____

15

> 저 학생들은 내 반 친구들이다.
> (classmate)

➡ _____

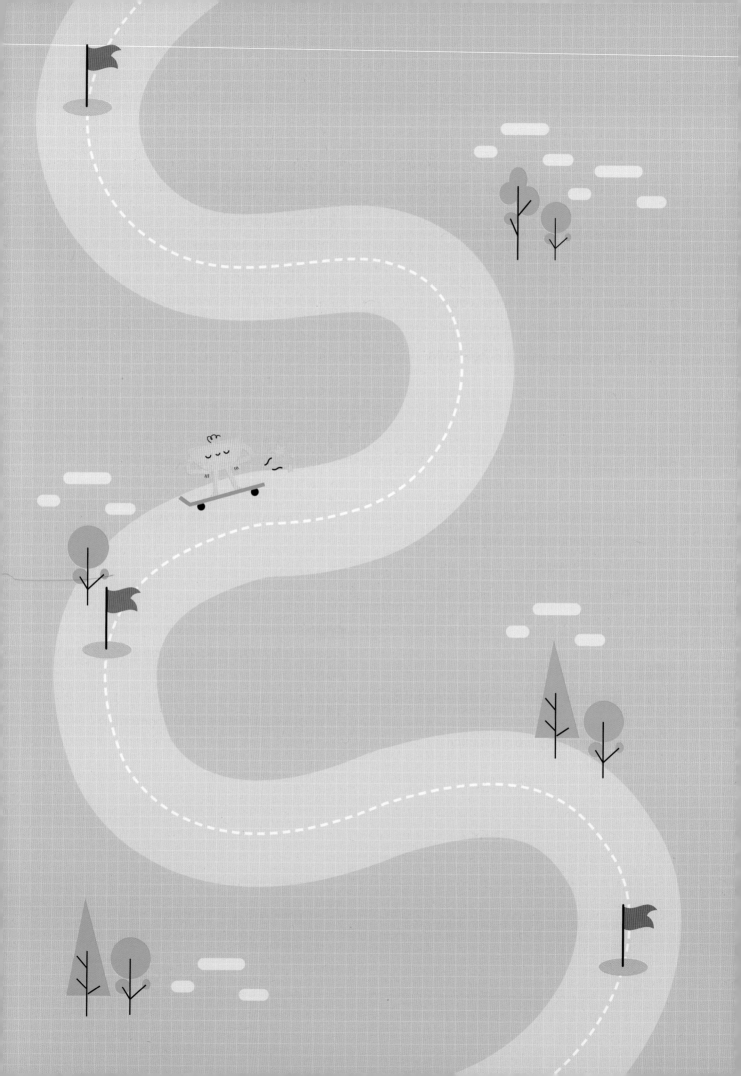

03

There & It

학습목표

1   There is / are 구문에 대해 알아보고 부정문과 의문문을 만드는 방법을 익혀요.

2   비인칭 주어 It의 쓰임에 대해 알아봐요.

UNIT 01 There is / are

1 긍정문

There is a cat on the sofa.

There are two dogs in the car.

There + be동사		
There is	There is *a tree* in the garden. There is *milk* in the refrigerator.	정원에 나무 한 그루가 있다. 냉장고에 우유가 있다.
There are	There are *six buttons* on my shirt. There are *many people* at the bus stop.	내 셔츠에 단추 여섯 개가 있다. 버스 정류장에 많은 사람들이 있다.

☑ **There is / are** 구문은 '~이 있다'라고 말할 때 사용해요. **There is** 뒤에는 **단수 주어**가, **There are** 뒤에는 **복수 주어**가 와요.

☑ **셀 수 없는 명사**는 양에 상관 없이 항상 단수 취급하므로 **There is**와 써야 해요.

　e.g. There *are* some butter on the plate. (X)　　There *is* some butter on the plate. (O)

PRACTICE 1　There is / are 넣기

① ___There___ ___is___ a ruler on the desk.

② _____ _____ ten books on the shelf.

③ _____ _____ some water in the bottle.

④ _____ _____ some coins in my pocket.

2 부정문 / 의문문

Is there a bookstore near here?

No, there isn't.

문장의 종류		
부정문	There is not[isn't] a tree in the garden. There are not[aren't] any chairs in my bedroom.	정원에 나무가 없다. 내 침실에 의자가 없다.
의문문	Is there a movie theater near here? Are there many people on the bus?	이 근처에 극장이 있나요? 버스에 사람이 많이 있나요?

☑ be동사 뒤에 not을 붙이면 '~이 없다'라는 뜻의 부정문이 돼요.

☑ be동사와 there의 위치를 바꾸고 문장 끝에 물음표(?)를 붙이면 '~이 있나요?'라는 뜻의 의문문이 돼요.

PRACTICE 2 문장 연결하기

❶ Is there •   • an elevator in this building.

❷ There isn't •   • a clock on the wall?

❸ Are there •   • any pencils in my pencil case.

❹ There aren't •   • any dogs in the park?

A 빈칸에 is와 are 중에서 알맞은 말을 골라 쓰세요.

1 There ___is___ a computer on the desk.

2 There _____ three schools in this town.

3 There _____ a lighthouse on the beach.

4 There _____ three bathrooms in the building.

5 There _____ a café on King Street.

6 There _____ a parrot in the cage.

7 There _____ zebras in the grass.

8 There _____ some money in my wallet.

9 There _____ many cars on the street.

10 There _____ two windows in this room.

11 There _____ a photo of my family on the wall.

12 There _____ seven days in a week.

13 There _____ a lot of food on the table.

14 There _____ some fish in the aquarium.

15 There _____ an Italian restaurant near here.

WORDS **town** 마을　**lighthouse** 등대　**bathroom** 욕실, 화장실　**café** 카페　**parrot** 앵무새　**cage** 새장, 우리　**zebra** 얼룩말　**grass** 풀, 잔디(밭)　**wallet** 지갑　**photo** 사진　**a lot of** 많은　**aquarium** 수족관

B ( ) 안에서 알맞은 것을 고르세요.

1 There (is, are) a bank on the corner.

2 (Is, Are) there a parking lot near here?

3 There (isn't, aren't) any flowers in the vase.

4 (Is, Are) there any ice cream in the refrigerator?

5 There (is, are) many hotels in big cities.

6 There (is, are) a calendar on the wall.

7 There (isn't, aren't) a cloud in the sky.

8 (Is, Are) there any children in the park?

9 (Is, Are) there any water in the glass?

10 There (is, are) two new students in our class.

11 (Is, Are) there many museums in London?

12 (Is, Are) there a gym in your school?

13 There (isn't, aren't) many people at the party.

14 There (is, are) a big cat in the jewelry store.

15 There (isn't, aren't) a good movie on TV tonight.

 WORDS on the corner 길모퉁이에   parking lot 주차장   vase 꽃병   refrigerator 냉장고   calendar 달력
cloud 구름   museum 박물관   gym 체육관   jewelry store 보석 가게

영작 술술

A 우리말과 같은 뜻이 되도록 빈칸에 알맞은 말을 쓰세요.

1 내 양말에 구멍 하나가 있다.

➡ ___There___ ___is___ a hole in my sock.

2 놀이터에 아이들 다섯 명이 있다.

➡ _____ _____ five children on the playground.

3 찻주전자에 차가 약간 있다.

➡ _____ _____ some tea in the teapot.

4 이 근처에는 큰 쇼핑몰이 없다.

➡ _____ _____ a big shopping mall near here.

5 병에 물이 조금도 없다.

➡ _____ _____ any water in the bottle.

6 냉장고에 달걀이 조금도 없다.

➡ _____ _____ any eggs in the refrigerator.

7 8시에 기차가 있나요?

➡ _____ _____ a train at 8 o'clock?

8 그 공연 표가 좀 있나요?

➡ _____ _____ any tickets for the show?

9 제 작문에 실수가 많이 있나요?

➡ _____ _____ many mistakes in my writing?

10 빵에 버터가 너무 많이 있나요?

➡ _____ _____ too much butter on your bread?

B 주어진 말을 이용하여 우리말을 영어로 바꿔 쓰세요. (부정문은 줄임말을 쓸 것)

1 당신에게 온 선물이 하나 있다. (gift, for you)

➡ There is a gift for you.

2 유리잔에 우유가 약간 있다. (some, in the glass)

➡ _____

3 그 집에는 침실이 세 개가 있다. (bedroom, in the house)

➡ _____

4 주차장에 차가 없다. (a car)

➡ _____

5 내 커피에는 설탕이 조금도 없다. (any, in my coffee)

➡ _____

6 그 상점에는 사람들이 많이 있지 않다. (many, in the shop)

➡ _____

7 이 근처에 수영장이 있나요? (a swimming pool)

➡ _____

8 정원에 꽃이 많이 있나요? (many, in the garden)

➡ _____

9 식탁 위에 음식이 좀 있나요? (any, on the table)

➡ _____

10 당신의 나라에는 산이 많이 있나요? (many, in your country)

➡ _____

TIP 1

There is 뒤에는 단수 주어가, There are 뒤에는 복수 주어가 와요. 단, 셀 수 없는 명사는 단수 취급하므로 There is와 함께 써야 해요.

e.g.
- There is an apple.
- There are apples.
- There is some food.

TIP 2

any는 부정문과 의문문에서 자주 쓰여요. 부정문에서는 '조금도, 아무것도', 의문문에서는 '얼마간의, 무슨'의 뜻이에요.

e.g.
- There isn't any water in the glass.
- Are there any books on the table?

WRAP UP

A　Grammar　밑줄 친 부분을 바르게 고쳐 문장을 다시 쓰세요.

1　<u>There are</u> a hair in my soup.　→　There is a hair in my soup.

2　<u>There is</u> some people outside.　→　_____

3　<u>There are</u> a woman at the door.　→　_____

4　<u>Are there</u> a flight at 7:30?　→　_____

5　<u>There are</u> a lot of rice in the jar.　→　_____

6　<u>Is there</u> any problems with it?　→　_____

7　<u>There isn't</u> any books in the bag.　→　_____

B　Writing　주어진 말을 이용하여 우리말을 영어로 바꿔 쓰세요.

1　종이 위에 개미 한 마리가 있다. (on the paper)

➡　There is an ant on the paper.

2　선반 위에 책들이 조금도 없다. (any, on the shelf)

➡　_____

3　공항 가는 버스가 있습니까? (bus to the airport)

➡　_____

4　바닥에 물이 많이 있다. (a lot of, on the floor)

➡　_____

5　너의 마을에는 공원이 많이 있니? (many, in your town)

➡　_____

C 내신 대비 질문을 읽고, 알맞은 답을 고르세요.

1 There is와 There are 중에서 빈칸에 들어갈 말이 <u>다른</u> 하나는?

① _____ people on the bus.

② _____ socks in the drawer.

③ _____ potatoes on the table.

④ _____ some snow on the roof.

2 우리말을 영어로 바르게 옮긴 것은?

> 집 옆에 자동차 한 대가 있다.

① Their is a car next to the house.

② They're a car next to the house.

③ There is a car next to the house.

④ There are a car next to the house.

개념 Review

아래 빈칸을 채우면서 개념을 다시 한번 익혀보세요.

❶ **There is / are 긍정문**

☑ There is / are 구문은 '~이 있다'라고 말할 때 사용해요. There is 뒤에는 ❶ _____ 가, There are 뒤에는 ❷ _____ 가 와요.

☑ 셀 수 없는 명사는 양에 상관 없이 항상 단수 취급하므로 ❸ _____ 와 써야 해요.

❷ **There is / are 부정문 / 의문문**

☑ be동사 뒤에 ❹ _____ 을 붙이면 '~이 없다'라는 뜻의 부정문이 돼요.

☑ be동사와 ❺ _____ 의 위치를 바꾸고 문장 끝에 물음표(?)를 붙이면 '~이 있나요?'라는 뜻의 의문문이 돼요.

비인칭 주어 It

1 시간 / 날짜 / 요일

Let's hurry. **It's** 9 o'clock.

It's October 31.

It의 쓰임		
시간	**It** is 7 o'clock. **It** is 10:30.	7시이다. 10시 30분이다.
날짜	**It** is December 31. **It** is my birthday today.	12월 31일이다. 오늘은 내 생일이다.
요일	**It** is Monday.	월요일이다.

☑ **시간, 날짜, 요일**에 대해 말할 때는 **비인칭 주어 it**을 사용해요. 이때 it은 형식적인 주어로 '그것'이라고 해석하지 않아요.

PRACTICE 1 알맞은 말 고르기

❶ (It, There) is August 3 today.

❷ (It, There) is only 6 o'clock.

❸ (It, There) is a lamp on the table.

❹ Was (it, there) Jane's birthday yesterday?

2 날씨 / 계절 / 거리

It is very cold today.

It is summer.

It의 쓰임		
날씨	It is raining. It is sunny and clear. It is a nice day today.	비가 내리고 있다. 날씨가 화창하고 맑다. 오늘은 날씨가 좋다.
계절	It is spring / summer / fall / winter.	봄 / 여름 / 가을 / 겨울이다.
거리	It is 3 kilometers from here to school. It is a 10-minute walk to the station.	여기서 학교까지 3킬로미터이다. 역까지 걸어서 10분 거리이다.

☑ 날씨, 계절, 거리에 대해 말할 때도 **비인칭 주어 it**을 사용해요.

PRACTICE 2 알맞은 말 고르기

❶ Look! (It, There) is snowing outside.

❷ (It, There) is a beautiful river in my town.

❸ In Korea, (it, there) rains a lot in July.

❹ (It, There) is not far from here to the park.

A ( ) 안에서 알맞은 것을 고르세요.

1 (It is, There is) 12 o'clock now.

2 (It is, There is) a train at 6:30.

3 (It is, There is) 2 kilometers from my house to school.

4 In Korea, (it is, there is) hot and humid in summer.

5 (Is it, Is there) far from here to the theater?

6 (It was, There was) a nice day yesterday.

7 (It is, There is) a national holiday this month.

8 (It was, There was) Aunt Marie's birthday yesterday.

9 (It was, There was) heavy rain last night.

10 (Is it, Is there) windy outside?

11 (It is, There is) going to be sunny tomorrow.

12 (Is it, Is there) Tuesday or Wednesday?

13 (It is, There is) a present under the Christmas tree.

14 (It is, There is) April, but the weather is still cold.

15 (It is, There is) only one kilometer to the park.

 WORDS kilometer 킬로미터 **from A to B** A부터 B까지 **humid** 습한 **far** (거리가) 먼 **theater** 극장
national holiday 국경일 **heavy rain** 폭우 **windy** 바람이 많이 부는 **Tuesday** 화요일
Wednesday 수요일 **present** 선물 **under** ~ 아래에 **April** 4월 **still** 여전히

B 빈칸에 it과 there 중에서 알맞은 말을 골라 쓰세요.

1 _____It_____ is September 15.

2 _____ is a policeman in that car.

3 Is _____ snowing outside?

4 _____ is Children's Day today.

5 Is _____ a dog in the house?

6 _____ is Monday, and tomorrow is my birthday.

7 In summer, _____ rains a lot in my country.

8 _____ is cold inside the room.

9 _____ is a big pond in the middle of the park.

10 _____ is 10:30 in China now.

11 _____ is fall, and the air is cool.

12 _____ is not far from here. Let's walk.

13 _____ is a strong wind outside.

14 _____ was very foggy this morning.

15 _____ is the first day of school.

 WORDS September 9월   Children's Day 어린이날   a lot 많이   inside ~안에   pond 연못
in the middle of ~의 중앙에   air 공기   let's ~하자   strong wind 강풍   foggy 안개가 낀
first 첫째의; 첫째

영작 술술

A 우리말과 같은 뜻이 되도록 빈칸에 알맞은 말을 쓰세요.

1 11시 30분이다.

→ _____It_____ _____is_____ 11:30.

2 지난 주말은 날씨가 화창했다.

→ _____ _____ sunny last weekend.

3 오늘은 화요일이 아니다.

→ _____ _____ _____ Tuesday today.

4 오후 3시이다.

→ _____ _____ 3 o'clock in the afternoon.

5 작년 겨울에 눈이 많이 왔다.

→ _____ _____ a lot last winter.

6 나의 부모님의 결혼기념일이다.

→ _____ _____ my parents' wedding anniversary.

7 여기서 공항까지 먼가요?

→ _____ _____ far from here to the airport?

8 어제는 당신의 생일이었나요?

→ _____ _____ your birthday yesterday?

9 우체국까지 걸어서 5분 거리이다.

→ _____ _____ a 5-minute walk to the post office.

10 오늘은 그다지 덥지 않다.

→ _____ _____ _____ very hot today.

B 주어진 말과 it을 이용하여 우리말을 영어로 바꿔 쓰세요.

1 6월 10일이다. (June 10)

→   It is June 10.

2 5시밖에 되지 않았다. (only)

→

3 벌써 가을이다. (already)

→

4 여기서 버스 정류장까지 1킬로미터이다. (the bus stop)

→

5 오늘이 목요일인가요? (Thursday today)

→

6 날씨가 화창하고 따뜻하다. (sunny, warm)

→

TIP 1

날짜는 다음과 같이
나타낼 수 있어요.

e.g.
- It is April 1.
- It is the first of April.

7 내일이 11월 1일인가요? (November 1)

→

8 어제는 Gina의 생일이었다. (Gina's birthday yesterday)

→

TIP 2

날씨를 나타낼 때는 it
뒤에 다양한 표현을 쓸 수
있어요.

e.g.
- It is cloudy.
  날씨가 흐리다.
- It is raining.
  (지금) 비가 오고 있다.
- It snows a lot here.
  이곳은 눈이 많이 내린다.

9 런던에는 비가 매우 자주 내린다. (rain, London, very often)

→

10 공항까지 운전으로 두 시간 거리이다. (two-hour drive, to, airport)

→

WRAP UP

A Grammar 밑줄 친 부분을 바르게 고쳐 문장을 다시 쓰세요.

1 <u>Its</u> time to go home. ➡ It's time to go home.

2 <u>Is this</u> 7:30 now? ➡ _____

3 It <u>isn't</u> foggy yesterday. ➡ _____

4 <u>This is</u> a nice day today. ➡ _____

5 <u>There is</u> raining outside. ➡ _____

6 <u>This doesn't</u> snow in Taiwan. ➡ _____

7 <u>That is not</u> Friday today. ➡ _____

B Writing 주어진 말과 it을 이용하여 우리말을 영어로 바꿔 쓰세요.

1 밖은 매우 흐리다. (cloudy, outside)

➡ It is very cloudy outside.

2 벌써 7시이다. (already)

➡ _____

3 어제는 비가 내리지 않았다. (rain)

➡ _____

4 오늘이 10월 1일인가요? (October 1 today)

➡ _____

5 그 공원까지 걸어서 30분 거리이다. (a 30-minute walk, to)

➡ _____

C 내신 대비 질문을 읽고, 알맞은 답을 고르세요.

1 밑줄 친 it의 쓰임이 다른 하나는?

① It is only 2 o'clock.

② It was cold last night.

③ It is a very interesting movie.

④ It is 1.5 kilometers to the museum.

2 우리말을 영어로 바르게 옮긴 것은?

> 우리 집에서 그 영화관까지 멀지 않다.

① Its not far from my house to the movie theater.

② It isn't far from my house to the movie theater.

③ This isn't far from my house to the movie theater.

④ There isn't far from my house to the movie theater.

개념 Review

아래 빈칸을 채우면서 개념을 다시 한번 익혀보세요.

❶ 시간 / 날짜 / 요일의 주어

☑ 시간, 날짜, 요일에 대해 말할 때는 ❶   주어 ❷   을 사용해요. 이때 it은
형식적인 주어로 ' ❸   '이라고 해석하지 않아요.

❷ 날씨 / 계절 / 거리의 주어

☑ 날씨, 계절, 거리에 대해 말할 때도 비인칭 주어 ❹   을 사용해요.

[01-02] 대화의 빈칸에 알맞은 말을 고르시오.

01

| A _____ a bookstore near here? |
| B Yes. It is on Ray Street. |

① Is it

② Is there

③ Are they

④ Are there

02

| A Do you have the time? |
| B Yes. _____ 2 o'clock now. |

① Its

② It is

③ This is

④ There is

03 빈칸에 들어갈 말로 알맞지 <u>않은</u> 것은?

| There are _____ on the table. |

① apples

② five books

③ some cheese

④ two glasses of water

04 밑줄 친 it의 쓰임이 <u>다른</u> 하나는?

① <u>It</u> is 5 o'clock.

② <u>It</u> is March 13.

③ <u>It</u> is my notebook.

④ <u>It</u> is a beautiful day.

05 빈칸에 들어갈 말이 순서대로 바르게 짝지어진 것은?

| _____ spring. _____ many flowers in the garden. |

① Its – There is

② It is – There is

③ It is – There are

④ This is – There are

서술형

06 두 문장이 같은 뜻이 되도록 할 때 빈칸에 알맞은 말을 쓰시오.

| Three students are in the classroom. |

➡ _____ _____ three students in the classroom.

07 밑줄 친 부분의 쓰임이 <u>어색한</u> 것은?

| <u>There</u> <u>are</u> <u>a lot of</u> <u>bread</u> on the plate.
  ①   ②   ③   ④ |

[08-09] 다음 중 <u>틀린</u> 문장을 고르시오.

08 ① There isn't any time for us.

② There are two men in that car.

③ Is there any peaches in the refrigerator?

④ There are too many cars on the road.

09 ① It is 6:30 now.

② Is it your birthday?

③ It is cold and dry today.

④ It isn't rain a lot in winter.

서술형

[10-11] 우리말과 같은 뜻이 되도록 주어진 말을 바르게 배열하시오.

10

서랍 안에 펜이 좀 있나요?
(there / pens / in / any / the drawer / are)

➡ _____

11

우리 집에서 그 병원까지 5킬로미터 거리이다.
(from / to / 5 kilometers / it / my house / the hospital / is)

➡ _____

[12-13] 우리말을 영어로 바르게 옮긴 것을 고르시오.

12

책상 위에 연필 두 자루와 자 한 개가 있다.

① There is pencil and ruler on the desk.

② There is two pencils and a ruler on the desk.

③ There are two pencils and ruler on the desk.

④ There are two pencils and a ruler on the desk.

13

그 나라에는 눈이 많이 내리나요?

① Is it snow a lot in the country?

② Does it snow a lot in the country?

③ Is there snow a lot in the country?

④ Are there snow a lot in the country?

서술형

[14-15] <u>틀린</u> 부분을 바르게 고쳐 문장을 다시 쓰시오.

14

Is there many people in the mall?

➡ _____

15

There is warm and sunny today.

➡ _____

04

형용사

학습목표

1 형용사의 역할과 형용사가 명사, 동사와 어떻게 함께 쓰이는지 알아봐요.

2 수량형용사의 종류와 쓰임에 대해 알아봐요.

UNIT 01 형용사의 쓰임

1 형용사+명사

That is a **tall** building.

They are **colorful** houses.

형용사+명사	They live in a **big** *house*. She has a **bright** *smile*. Jake likes his **old** *bike*. Ann is wearing a **purple** *dress*. He visited many **different** *countries*.	그들은 큰 집에 산다. 그녀는 밝은 미소를 갖고 있다. Jake는 그의 오래된 자전거를 좋아한다. Ann은 자주색 원피스를 입고 있다. 그는 많은 다른 나라들을 방문했다.

☑ **형용사**는 **명사 앞**에서 명사를 꾸며주는 역할을 해요. **e.g. a girl → a pretty girl**

☑ 형용사를 사용하면 명사에 대해 더 구체적으로 설명할 수 있어요.

PRACTICE 1   알맞은 형용사 넣기

> cold   old   dirty   difficult

❶ I hate _____cold_____ weather.

❷ He asked me a _____ question.

❸ She cleaned the _____ dishes.

❹ They crossed an _____ bridge.

2 동사+형용사

My dog is **big**.

My cat is **small**.

be동사+형용사	I *am* **happy**. The room *is* **dark**.	나는 행복하다. 그 방은 어둡다.
감각동사+형용사	I *feel* **tired**. You *look* **angry**. The perfume *smells* **good**. This milk *tastes* **sour**. That *sounds* **interesting**.	나는 피곤함을 느낀다. 너는 화가 나 보인다. 그 향수는 좋은 냄새가 난다. 이 우유는 신맛이 난다. 그것은 흥미롭게 들린다.

☑ 형용사는 be동사나 feel / look / smell / taste / sound처럼 감각과 관련한 동사 뒤에 쓰여요.

☑ 형용사가 동사 뒤에 쓰이면 **주어의 상태**를 나타내요.

PRACTICE 2 알맞은 형용사 넣기

| beautiful | big | fast | salty |

❶ Elephants are _____big_____.

❷ The airplane is _____.

❸ Seawater tastes _____.

❹ Her song sounds _____.

A 문장에서 형용사에 <u>모두</u> 동그라미 하세요.

1 The man is a (famous) writer.

2 They visited an old castle.

3 These oranges are fresh.

4 We had a hot summer this year.

5 The chicken smells delicious.

6 The boy is reading a thick book.

7 This medicine tastes bitter.

8 The girl has colorful balloons.

9 I look ugly in this photo.

10 Snakes are dangerous animals.

11 This pumpkin is big.

12 Bob is wearing a long shirt and shorts.

13 We had a wonderful time on our vacation.

14 The new sofa looks comfortable.

15 This blanket feels warm and soft.

---

 writer 작가　**castle** 성　**chicken** 닭, 닭고기　**thick** 두꺼운　**medicine** 약　**bitter** (맛이) 쓴
colorful 형형색색의, 다채로운　**balloon** 풍선　**ugly** 못생긴, 추한　**pumpkin** 호박　**shorts** 반바지
comfortable 편안한　**blanket** 담요　**soft** 부드러운, 푹신한

B 주어진 형용사가 들어갈 위치로 알맞은 곳에 V표 하세요.

1   This is an book. (interesting)

2   Robert is happy with his job. (new)

3   She writes songs. (beautiful)

4   Jane looks today. (lovely)

5   Mr. Brown is to people. (kind)

6   Linda brushed her hair. (long)

7   Turtles are runners. (slow)

8   The students felt after the exam. (tired)

9   My uncle has a very dog. (clever)

10   Susan bought a table. (round)

11   Your idea sounds. (good)

12   Science class is for me. (difficult)

13   Tomatoes are a food. (healthy)

14   Nurses help people. (sick)

15   She put the money in a place. (safe)

 WORDS lovely 사랑스러운, 예쁜   brush one's hair 머리를 빗다   turtle 거북이   clever 영리한   round 둥근
healthy 건강한, 건강에 좋은   nurse 간호사   sick 아픈   safe 안전한   place 장소, 곳

A 우리말과 같은 뜻이 되도록 빈칸에 알맞은 말을 쓰세요.

1   그것은 큰 실수였다.

→ It was ___a___ ___big___ mistake .

2   기린은 긴 목을 갖고 있다.

→ The giraffe has _____ _____ _____ .

3   그녀는 파란색 코트를 입고 있다.

→ She is wearing _____ _____ _____ .

4   그 사다리는 안전하다.

→ The ladder _____ _____ .

5   그 계획은 흥미롭게 들린다.

→ The plan _____ _____ .

6   그 베개는 푹신하고(부드럽고) 편안하다.

→ The pillow is _____ and _____ .

7   그 배낭은 무거워 보인다.

→ The backpack _____ _____ .

8   그의 농담은 항상 재미있다(웃기다).

→ His jokes _____ always _____ .

9   그 스테이크는 맛이 좋지 않다.

→ The steak doesn't _____ g_____ .

10   그 아이들은 무서움을 느꼈다.

→ The children _____ s_____ .

B 주어진 말을 이용하여 우리말을 영어로 바꿔 쓰세요.

1 그는 친절한 사람이다. (person)

→ He is a kind person.

2 야구는 인기 있는 스포츠이다. (baseball, popular)

→

3 너는 오늘 예뻐 보인다. (lovely)

→

4 그것은 지루한 영화였다. (boring)

→

5 이 방은 작고 지저분하다. (this room, dirty)

→

6 그 젊은 사업가는 부유하다. (businessman, rich)

→

7 우리는 지루함을 느꼈다. (bored)

→

8 그는 두 개의 다른 나라에서 살았다. (live in, different country)

→

9 그 다크 초콜릿은 쓴 맛이 난다. (dark chocolate, bitter)

→

10 그 자동차 엔진은 부드러운 소리가 난다. (car engine, smooth)

→

TIP 1

관사, 수를 나타내는 말, 소유격 등은 「형용사 + 명사」 앞에 위치해요.

e.g.
- a good boy
- two red shirts
- his new car

TIP 2

boring은 어떤 상황이나 사물이 '지루하다'라고 말할 때 쓰고, bored는 무언가에 의해 사람이 지루함을 느낄 때 써요.

e.g.
- The class is boring.
- I am bored.

WRAP UP

A Grammar 주어진 형용사를 넣어 문장을 다시 쓰세요.

1 This watch is too. (expensive) → This watch is too expensive.

2 He has a cat. (white) → _____

3 Beth looks today. (sad) → _____

4 That is an idea. (interesting) → _____

5 Bob sold his car. (old) → _____

6 The tower is very. (tall) → _____

7 My mom's soup tastes. (great) → _____

B Writing 주어진 말을 이용하여 우리말을 영어로 바꿔 쓰세요.

1 그 잔은 비어있다. (the glass)

→ The glass is empty. _____

2 우리에게는 충분한 돈이 없다. (have, enough)

→ _____

3 너의 영어는 매우 훌륭하다. (very good)

→ _____

4 그 노부부는 행복해 보인다. (old couple)

→ _____

5 그 축제는 지루했다. (festival)

→ _____

C 내신 대비 질문을 읽고, 알맞은 답을 고르세요.

1 다음 중 문장이 틀린 것은?

① The show was funny.

② I met a famous singer.

③ The bridge looks danger.

④ I didn't feel comfortable.

2 우리말을 영어로 바르게 옮긴 것은?

> 새로 오신 영어 선생님은 매우 친절하다.

① The English new teacher is kind very.

② The English teacher new is very kind.

③ The new English teacher is very kind.

④ The new English teacher is kind very.

개념 Review

아래 빈칸을 채우면서 개념을 다시 한번 익혀보세요.

❶ 형용사 + 명사

☑ 형용사는 명사 ❶ _____ 에서 명사를 꾸며주는 역할을 해요.

☑ 형용사를 사용하면 명사에 대해 더 구체적으로 설명할 수 있어요.

❷ 동사 + 형용사

☑ 형용사는 ❷ _____ 나 feel / look / smell / taste / sound처럼 ❸ _____ 과 관련한
동사 뒤에 쓰여요.

☑ 형용사가 동사 뒤에 쓰이면 주어의 ❹ _____ 를 나타내요.

UNIT 02 수량형용사

1 many / much / a lot of

She reads **many** books.

She didn't buy **much** food.

수량형용사		
many＋셀 수 있는 명사의 복수형	I have **many** *friends*.	나는 친구가 많다.
much＋셀 수 없는 명사	We don't have **much** *time*.	우리는 시간이 많지 않다.
a lot of＋ 셀 수 있는 명사의 복수형 / 셀 수 없는 명사	He reads **a lot of** *books*. She bought **a lot of** *food*.	그는 많은 책을 읽는다. 그녀는 많은 음식을 샀다.

- ☑ 수나 양이 '**많은**'의 의미는 **many, much, a lot of**를 사용해요.
- ☑ **many**는 셀 수 있는 명사의 복수형 앞, **much**는 셀 수 없는 명사 앞에 사용해요.
- ☑ **a lot of**는 셀 수 있는 명사와 셀 수 없는 명사 앞에 모두 사용할 수 있어요.

PRACTICE 1 many / much 넣어 문장 다시 쓰기

❶ Did you buy <u>a lot of</u> food?   →   <u>Did you buy much food?</u>

❷ I ate <u>a lot of</u> apples.   →   _____

❸ He doesn't have <u>a lot of</u> money.   →   _____

❹ Did you take <u>a lot of</u> pictures?   →   _____

2 some / any

I have **some** cookies.

He doesn't eat **any** vegetables.

문장의 종류	수량형용사		
긍정문	some	He has **some** *pens*. He has **some** *money*.	그는 펜 몇 개가 있다. 그는 돈이 약간 있다.
부정문	any	He doesn't have **any** *pens*. He doesn't have **any** *money*.	그는 펜이 하나도 없다. 그는 돈이 조금도 없다.
의문문	any	Does he have **any** *pens*? Does he have **any** *money*?	그는 펜이 좀 있나요? 그는 돈이 좀 있나요?

☑ '**약간의, 조금의(몇몇의)**'라는 의미는 some과 any를 사용해요. some과 any는 셀 수 있는 명사와 셀 수 없는 명사 앞에 모두 쓸 수 있어요.

☑ some은 **긍정문**에, any는 **부정문**과 **의문문**에 사용해요.

PRACTICE 2 some / any 넣기

❶ I have ____some____ books in my bag.

❷ Do you need _____ help?

❸ It's cold. I want _____ hot soup.

❹ Jessica doesn't eat _____ meat.

 문법 쏙쏙

A ( ) 안에서 알맞은 것을 고르세요.

1　He wrote (many, much) poems.

2　We don't have (many, much) time.

3　We got (many, a lot of) snow this winter.

4　He visited (a lot of, much) different countries.

5　The children make too (many, much) noise.

6　We saw (a lot of, much) animals at the zoo.

7　Our teacher gives us (many, a lot of) homework.

8　(Many, Much) people go to the beach in summer.

9　Bob knows (a lot of, much) songs.

10　I made (many, much) mistakes on my test.

11　Jimmy drinks too (many, much) soda.

12　Liz reads (a lot of, much) books in her free time.

13　Rome has (many, much) beautiful buildings.

14　Do you drink (many, a lot of) water every day?

15　There are so (many, much) stars in the sky.

WORDS　poem 시　**make noise** 시끄럽게 하다　**zoo** 동물원　**soda** 탄산음료　**free time** 여가[자유] 시간　**star** 별

B 밑줄 친 부분이 맞으면 OK라고 쓰고, **틀리면** 바르게 고치세요.

1　There is <u>any</u> food on the table.　　➡　　some

2　Do you have <u>any</u> problems?　　➡　　_____

3　I don't need <u>some</u> help right now.　　➡　　_____

4　Margaret wants to buy <u>any</u> shoes.　　➡　　_____

5　Are there <u>some</u> messages for me?　　➡　　_____

6　She put <u>any</u> sugar in her coffee.　　➡　　_____

7　<u>Some</u> students failed the exam.　　➡　　_____

8　Do you have <u>any</u> plans for the weekend?　　➡　　_____

9　John has <u>any</u> chocolate in his bag.　　➡　　_____

10　She drinks <u>some</u> tea after lunch.　　➡　　_____

11　He doesn't eat <u>some</u> carrots.　　➡　　_____

12　Ella put <u>some</u> butter on her bread.　　➡　　_____

13　There are <u>any</u> cherries in the bowl.　　➡　　_____

14　Do you have <u>some</u> chairs for me?　　➡　　_____

15　Mr. Smith is eating <u>some</u> fruit.　　➡　　_____

WORDS help 도움; 돕다　message 메시지　fail (시험에) 떨어지다, 낙제하다　plan 계획　weekend 주말
cherry 체리

영작 술술

A 우리말과 같은 뜻이 되도록 빈칸에 알맞은 말을 쓰세요.

1 나는 몇 편의 영화를 보았다.

→ I watched ___some___ ___movies___ .

2 그는 물을 많이 마신다.

→ He drinks _____ _____ _____ _____ .

3 거리에 많은 사람들이 있다.

→ There are _____ _____ on the street.

4 그들은 할 일이 너무 많이 있다.

→ They have too _____ _____ to do.

5 나는 그녀에게 꽃들을 좀 보냈다.

→ I sent her _____ _____ .

6 그는 친구들이 하나도 없다.

→ He doesn't have _____ _____ .

7 집에 우유가 많지 않다.

→ There isn't _____ _____ at home.

8 너는 어제 버터를 좀 샀니?

→ Did you buy _____ _____ yesterday?

9 Mary는 그녀의 생일에 많은 카드를 받았다.

→ Mary got _____ _____ on her birthday.

10 그는 TV 앞에서 많은 시간을 보낸다.

→ He spends _____ _____ _____ _____ in front of the TV.

B 주어진 말을 이용하여 우리말을 영어로 바꿔 쓰세요.

1 당신은 저축을 많이 합니까? (save, money)

→   Do you save much[a lot of] money?

2 우리는 많은 음식을 샀다. (buy, lot)

→ _____

3 나는 매달 몇 권의 책을 읽는다. (every month)

→ _____

4 너는 채소를 많이 먹니? (eat, vegetables)

→ _____

5 너는 형제나 자매가 좀 있니? (brothers or sisters)

→ _____

6 버스에 많은 사람들이 있다. (on the bus)

→ _____

7 그녀는 옷을 많이 산다. (clothes)

→ _____

8 나는 도움이 좀 필요하다. (help)

→ _____

9 Sandra는 여가 시간이 조금도 없다. (not, have, free time)

→ _____

10 접시에 치즈가 많이 있나요? (there, on the dish)

→ _____

TIP 1

much는 긍정문에서는 잘 쓰지 않고 대신 a lot of를 사용해요. much가 긍정문에 사용될 때는 부사 so, too 등과 같이 써요.

e.g.
- I have much work. (×)
- I have too much work. (○)
- I have a lot of work. (○)

TIP 2

some/any 뒤에 셀 수 있는 명사가 올 경우에는 반드시 복수형이어야 해요.

e.g.
- I have some books.
- Do you have any erasers?

WRAP UP

A Grammar 밑줄 친 부분을 바르게 고쳐 문장을 다시 쓰세요.

1 Some <u>student</u> passed the test. ➡ Some students passed the test.

2 I read <u>much books</u> on vacation. ➡ _____

3 We got <u>any snow</u> last winter. ➡ _____

4 He has too <u>many work</u> to do. ➡ _____

5 Are there <u>any gift</u> for me? ➡ _____

6 <u>Any people</u> went to the zoo. ➡ _____

7 He put <u>many salt</u> in the soup. ➡ _____

B Writing 주어진 말을 이용하여 우리말을 영어로 바꿔 쓰세요.

1 내 남동생은 장난감이 많다. (my little brother, toy)

➡ My little brother has many[a lot of] toys.

2 우리는 초콜릿을 많이 사지 않았다. (chocolate)

➡ _____

3 많은 학생들이 아팠다. (student, sick)

➡ _____

4 그 주스에는 설탕이 약간 있다. (sugar, in the juice)

➡ _____

5 그녀는 어떤 조언도 필요하지 않다. (need, advice)

➡ _____

C 내신 대비 질문을 읽고, 알맞은 답을 고르세요.

1 밑줄 친 부분이 올바른 것은?

① He has <u>much</u> friends.

② I ate <u>any</u> strawberries.

③ She bought <u>many</u> furniture.

④ There is <u>some</u> rice in the jar.

2 우리말을 영어로 바르게 옮긴 것은?

> 나는 운이 조금도 없었다.

① I didn't have a luck.

② I didn't have any luck.

③ I didn't have any lucks.

④ I didn't have some luck.

개념 Review

아래 빈칸을 채우면서 개념을 다시 한번 익혀보세요.

❶ **many / much / a lot of**
- ☑ 수나 양이 '많은'의 의미는 many, much, a lot of를 사용해요.
- ☑ ❶ ＿＿＿＿＿＿ 는 셀 수 있는 명사의 복수형 앞, ❷ ＿＿＿＿＿＿ 는 셀 수 없는 명사 앞에 사용해요.
- ☑ ❸ ＿＿＿＿＿＿ 는 셀 수 있는 명사와 셀 수 없는 명사 앞에 모두 사용할 수 있어요.

❷ **some / any**
- ☑ '약간의, 조금의(몇몇의)'라는 의미는 some과 any를 사용해요. some과 any는 셀 수 있는 명사와 셀 수 없는 명사 앞에 모두 쓸 수 있어요.
- ☑ ❹ ＿＿＿＿＿＿ 은 긍정문에, ❺ ＿＿＿＿＿＿ 는 부정문과 의문문에 사용해요.

[01-02] 대화의 빈칸에 알맞은 말을 고르시오.

01

> A Did you see Jane dancing?
> B Yes. She's a _____ dancer.

① very
② well
③ good
④ better

02

> A Are there eggs in the refrigerator?
> B Yes, but we don't have _____ milk.

① a
② some
③ many
④ much

03 다음 문장을 부정문으로 바꿀 때 빈칸에 들어갈 말로 알맞은 것은?

> Mary has some friends in London.
> ➡ Mary doesn't have _____ friends in London.

① a
② any
③ some
④ much

[04-05] 빈칸에 들어갈 말로 알맞지 <u>않은</u> 것을 고르시오.

04

> This soup _____ good.

① is
② has
③ smells
④ tastes

05

> She bought many _____.

① food
② books
③ apples
④ flowers

서술형

[06-07] 주어진 말을 이용하여 우리말을 영어로 바꿔 쓰시오.

06

> 농구 선수들은 키가 크다.
> (basketball player)

➡ _____

07

> 이 차는 좋은 냄새가 난다. (tea, good)

➡ _____

08 다음 중 밑줄 친 부분의 의미가 잘못 해석된 것은?

① Tony looked happy. (행복해 보였다)

② The chicken smelled delicious.
(맛있는 냄새가 났다)

③ The steak tasted strange.
(이상한 맛이 났다)

④ We all felt tired. (피곤하게 들렸다)

09 다음 밑줄 친 부분과 바꿔 쓸 수 있는 것은?

I saw a lot of movies last month.

① any
② some
③ many
④ much

[10-11] 다음 중 틀린 문장을 고르시오.

10 ① The man has a bag yellow.
② He carried a heavy suitcase.
③ Math is an interesting subject.
④ My mother is a very wise woman.

11 ① He ate too much cake.
② Many people like his songs.
③ Do you have any pets?
④ She didn't get some presents.

[12-13] 우리말을 영어로 바르게 옮긴 것을 고르시오.

12

그의 새 자전거는 비싸 보인다.

① His new bike looks expensive.
② His new bike expensive looks.
③ New his bike looks expensive.
④ His bike new looks expensive.

13

이 방에는 햇빛이 많지 않다.

① There is not any sunshine in this room.
② There is not some sunshine in this room.
③ There is not much sunshine in this room.
④ There is not many sunshine in this room.

서술형

[14-15] 틀린 부분을 바르게 고쳐 문장을 다시 쓰시오.

14

I usually have big a breakfast.

➡ _____

15

We saw some lion at the zoo.

➡ _____

05

부사

학습목표

1   부사의 역할과 형태에 대해 알아봐요.

2   빈도부사의 종류와 문장에서의 위치에 대해 알아봐요.

UNIT 01 부사의 쓰임

1 부사의 역할

He is playing the trumpet **loudly**.

The movie is **very** funny.

부사의 역할		
동사 수식	He *smiled* **kindly**.	그는 친절하게 웃었다.
형용사 수식	Jane is **very** *beautiful*.	Jane은 매우 아름답다.
다른 부사 수식	She speaks **so** *quietly*.	그녀는 아주 조용히 말한다.
문장 전체 수식	**Sadly**, *Jim lost the game*.	슬프게도, Jim은 그 경기에서 졌다.

☑ 부사는 **동사, 형용사, 다른 부사**, 또는 **문장 전체를 꾸며주는 역할**을 해요.

☑ 부사는 꾸며주는 동사의 앞 / 뒤, 형용사나 다른 부사의 앞, 문장의 앞 / 뒤에 위치해요.

PRACTICE 1 알맞은 부사 넣기

| very | luckily | brightly | slowly |

❶ The sun shines ___brightly___ .

❷ The movie is _____ sad.

❸ _____, he passed the exam.

❹ The snail moves very _____ .

2 부사의 형태

Ted is a **careful** driver. He drives **carefully**.

The man is running **fast**.

부사의 형태		
-ly로 끝나는 부사	bad 나쁜 – bad**ly** 나쁘게 nice 멋진 – nice**ly** 멋지게 quick 빠른 – quick**ly** 빠르게	quiet 조용한 – quiet**ly** 조용하게 careful 조심스러운 – careful**ly** 조심스럽게 beautiful 아름다운 – beautiful**ly** 아름답게
-ily로 끝나는 부사	easy 쉬운 – eas**ily** 쉽게 angry 화난 – angr**ily** 화나서	happy 행복한 – happ**ily** 행복하게 lucky 운이 좋은 – luck**ily** 운 좋게도
불규칙 부사	fast 빠른 – **fast** 빠르게 late 늦은 – **late** 늦게 early 이른 – **early** 이르게	high 높은 – **high** 높게 hard 열심히 하는 – **hard** 열심히 good 훌륭한 – **well** 잘

☑ 대부분의 부사는 형용사에 **-ly**를 붙여서 만들어요. 하지만 「자음 + y」로 끝나는 형용사는 **y를 i로 고치고 -ly**를 붙여요.

☑ 어떤 부사들은 형용사와 부사의 형태가 같거나 전혀 다르므로 주의해야 해요.

PRACTICE 2 형용사의 부사형 만들기

❶ kind → ___kindly___ ❺ great → _____

❷ easy → _____ ❻ strange → _____

❸ serious → _____ ❼ fast → _____

❹ angry → _____ ❽ good → _____

A ( ) 안에서 알맞은 것을 고르세요.

1 Mr. Taylor works very (hard, hardly).

2 Seoul is a very (safe, safely) city.

3 Joe hurt his ankle (bad, badly).

4 The children woke up (early, earily).

5 The horse runs (fast, fastly).

6 David was (late, lately) for the meeting.

7 (Sudden, Suddenly), a man came into the room.

8 He solved the problem (easy, easily).

9 I had a (strange, strangely) dream last night.

10 Anna dances (beautiful, beautifully).

11 The girl carried the glass jar (careful, carefully).

12 She looked very (angry, angrily).

13 It rained (heavy, heavily) yesterday.

14 The frog jumped (high, highly).

15 Air pollution is a (serious, seriously) problem.

 WORDS hurt 다치게 하다　ankle 발목　wake up (잠에서) 깨다　horse 말　suddenly 갑자기　come into ~로 들어오다　solve 풀다, 해결하다　dream 꿈; 꿈을 꾸다　jar 병, 단지　frog 개구리　jump 뛰어오르다 air pollution 대기 오염　serious 심각한, 진지한

B 주어진 말을 알맞은 형태로 고쳐 빈칸을 채우세요.

1 He made his bed __quickly__ . (quick)

2 My father snored _____ . (loud)

3 She climbed up the ladder _____ . (careful)

4 He greeted his teacher _____ . (polite)

5 The worker fixed the door _____ . (easy)

6 Susan speaks too _____ . (fast)

7 _____ , she didn't say anything. (strange)

8 Frank painted the picture _____ . (nice)

9 My kite is flying _____ in the sky. (high)

10 _____ , he didn't pass the test. (surprising)

11 Mr. Brown works _____ every day. (hard)

12 He got up _____ in the morning. (early)

13 Jane didn't sleep _____ last night. (good)

14 He shouted at me _____ . (angry)

15 They came back home _____ . (late)

 WORDS snore 코를 골다 climb up a ladder 사다리를 올라가다 greet 인사하다 polite 예의 바른, 정중한
fix 고치다 anything 무엇, 아무것 paint (물감으로) 그리다 nicely 멋지게, 잘 kite 연 surprising 놀라운
shout 소리치다

영작 술술

A 우리말과 같은 뜻이 되도록 빈칸에 알맞은 말을 쓰세요.

1 그는 문을 조용히 열었다.

   → He opened the door ___quietly___ .

2 그녀는 옷을 아름답게 입었다.

   → She dressed _____ .

3 Jack은 기타를 매우 잘 친다.

   → Jack plays the guitar very _____ .

4 그녀는 그 차를 조심스럽게 맛보았다.

   → She tasted the tea _____ .

5 Aaron은 너무 빨리 걷는다.

   → Aaron walks too _____ .

6 Tom은 그 질문에 쉽게 대답했다.

   → Tom answered the question _____ .

7 그 아이들은 안전하게 길을 건넜다.

   → The children crossed the street _____ .

8 그녀는 나를 슬프게 바라보았다.

   → She looked at me _____ .

9 나는 그 책들을 늦게 반납했다.

   → I returned the books _____ .

10 그들은 함께 행복하게 놀았다.

   → They played together _____ .

B 주어진 말을 이용하여 우리말을 영어로 바꿔 쓰세요.

1 나는 그 계란을 조심스럽게 깼다. (break)

➡ I broke the egg carefully.

2 그녀는 파티를 일찍 떠났다. (leave, party)

➡

3 운좋게도, 그는 그의 손목시계를 찾았다. (find, watch)

➡

4 그 버스가 늦게 도착했다. (arrive)

➡

5 그 학생은 그의 손을 높이 들었다. (raise one's hand)

➡

TIP 1

대부분의 부사는 형용사에 -ly를 붙여서 만들고, 「자음+y」로 끝나는 형용사는 y를 i로 고치고 -ly를 붙여요.

e.g.
- quiet – quietly
- easy – easily

6 그 기차는 갑자기 멈췄다. (stop)

➡

7 Minsu는 영어를 잘한다. (speak)

➡

8 Ruth는 그녀의 차를 빨리 운전한다. (drive one's car)

➡

TIP 2

어떤 부사들은 형용사와 형태가 같거나 전혀 다르므로 주의해야 해요.

e.g.
- He is a hard worker. (형용사)
  He works hard. (부사)
- She is a good cook. (형용사)
  She cooks well. (부사)

9 Jessica는 교실로 조용히 들어왔다. (come into, classroom)

➡

10 나의 할머니는 천천히 걸으셨다. (grandmother, walk)

➡

WRAP UP

A **Grammar** 밑줄 친 부분을 바르게 고쳐 문장을 다시 쓰세요.

1 Jack ate his lunch <u>quick</u>. ➡ Jack ate his lunch quickly.

2 The dog barks <u>loud</u>. ➡ _____

3 Paul is a <u>nicely</u> man. ➡ _____

4 Mike ran to school <u>fastly</u>. ➡ _____

5 The apple pie smells <u>deliciously</u>. ➡ _____

6 We all studied <u>hardly</u>. ➡ _____

7 James cooks very <u>good</u>. ➡ _____

B **Writing** 주어진 말을 이용하여 우리말을 영어로 바꿔 쓰세요.

1 Peter는 춤을 매우 잘 춘다. (dance)

➡ Peter dances very well.

2 그는 그 책을 큰 소리로 읽었다. (read)

➡ _____

3 그녀는 그 선물을 천천히 열어보았다. (open, present)

➡ _____

4 우리 팀은 경기를 못했다. (play, bad)

➡ _____

5 그들은 저녁을 늦게 먹었다. (eat one's dinner)

➡ _____

C [내신 대비] 질문을 읽고, 알맞은 답을 고르세요.

1 다음 중 형용사와 부사가 <u>잘못</u> 짝지어진 것은?

① heavy – heavily

② hard – hardly

③ good – well

④ late – late

2 밑줄 친 부분이 바르지 <u>않은</u> 것은?

① They did the exercise <u>easily</u>.

② Those people are very <u>kindly</u>.

③ She learns everything <u>quickly</u>.

④ He painted the kitchen <u>beautifully</u>.

개념 Review

아래 빈칸을 채우면서 개념을 다시 한번 익혀보세요.

❶ 부사의 역할

☑ 부사는 동사, 형용사, 다른 부사, 또는 문장 전체를 꾸며주는 역할을 해요.

☑ 부사는 꾸며주는 동사의 ❶   , 형용사나 다른 부사의 ❷   , 문장의

❸   에 위치해요.

❷ 부사의 형태

☑ 대부분의 부사는 형용사에 ❹   를 붙여서 만들어요. 하지만 「자음+y」로 끝나는 형용사는 y를

❺   로 고치고 ❻   를 붙여요.

☑ 어떤 부사들은 형용사와 부사의 형태가 같거나 전혀 다르므로 주의해야 해요.

UNIT 02 빈도부사

1 빈도부사의 종류

They **usually** play soccer.

Jack **never** does exercise.

빈도부사	의미		
always	항상	I **always** walk to school.	나는 항상 학교에 걸어간다.
usually	보통, 대개	He **usually** gets up at 7:30.	그는 보통 7시 30분에 일어난다.
often	자주, 종종	They **often** play tennis.	그들은 종종 테니스를 친다.
sometimes	가끔, 때때로	Ann **sometimes** goes hiking.	Ann은 때때로 하이킹하러 간다.
rarely	거의 ~않다	He **rarely** eats kimchi.	그는 거의 김치를 먹지 않는다.
never	결코 ~않다	You **never** clean your room.	너는 결코 네 방을 청소하지 않는다.

☑ **빈도부사**는 **횟수**를 나타내는 부사로 always(항상)부터 never(결코 ~않다)까지 다양한 종류가 있어요.

☑ **rarely**와 **never**는 이미 부정의 의미를 포함하기 때문에 not과 함께 쓸 수 없어요.

PRACTICE 1 빈도부사 넣기

❶ Fred는 항상 바쁘다.　　　→ Fred is ___always___ busy.

❷ 나는 보통 일찍 자러 간다.　→ I _____ go to bed early.

❸ 그는 종종 청바지를 입는다.　→ He _____ wears blue jeans.

❹ 그녀는 절대 화를 내지 않는다.　→ She _____ gets angry.

2 빈도부사의 위치

He **always** has breakfast.

He is **often** busy.

빈도부사의 위치		
일반동사 앞	She **usually** *arrives* early. He **rarely** *drinks* coffee.	그녀는 보통 일찍 도착한다. 그는 거의 커피를 마시지 않는다.
be동사 뒤	She *is* **always** happy. He *is* **sometimes** late for school.	그녀는 항상 행복하다. 그는 때때로 학교에 지각한다.
조동사 뒤	I *will* **never** make the same mistake.	나는 결코 같은 실수를 하지 않겠다.
의문문의 주어 뒤	Do *you* **often** eat out?	너는 종종 외식을 하니?

☑ 빈도부사는 **일반동사 앞, be동사나 조동사 뒤**에 위치해요.

☑ **의문문**에서는 빈도부사가 **주어 뒤**에 와요.

PRACTICE 2 빈도부사 넣기

❶ The ● man ✔ tells ● lies ● . (never)

❷ They ● are ● busy ● on ● Monday. (usually)

❸ My ● sister ● eats ● after ● 7:00 p.m. (rarely)

❹ Do ● you ● help ● your ● mother? (often)

문법 쏙쏙

A 주어진 빈도부사가 들어갈 위치로 알맞은 곳에 V표 하세요.

1   Jack ✓ has lunch at a restaurant. (often)

2   Eric fights with his friends. (never)

3   Our classroom is clean. (rarely)

4   Mrs. Lee is nice to her students. (usually)

5   We go shopping on Saturday afternoon. (often)

6   Do you feel sad? (sometimes)

7   My dog barks at people. (never)

8   I will visit you in New York. (sometimes)

9   He goes to the pool in the morning. (often)

10   I am nervous before interviews. (always)

11   I will forget your kindness. (never)

12   Is the school bus on time? (always)

13   Laura has ice cream for dessert. (usually)

14   Kate and James are cheerful. (always)

15   Peter leaves his cellphone on the table. (often)

 WORDS fight 싸우다   nice (사람이) 친절한, 좋은   bark 짖다   pool 수영장   nervous 불안한, 초조한   interview 면접
forget 잊다, 잊어버리다   kindness 친절   on time 정시에   cheerful 쾌활한   leave 두고 오다

B 주어진 말을 바르게 배열하여 문장을 완성하세요.

1 usually / a shower / in the morning / I / take / .

→   I usually take a shower in the morning.

2 surf / he / often / does / the Internet / ?

→ _____

3 is / a good student / Mike / always / .

→ _____

4 at midnight / go to / I / bed / usually / .

→ _____

5 she / fast food / never / eats / .

→ _____

6 crowded / the park / usually / is / ?

→ _____

7 takes / in the afternoon / sometimes / a nap / she / .

→ _____

8 do / I / the laundry / usually / on Saturday / .

→ _____

9 you / will / remember / always / I / .

→ _____

10 up / Tom / early / rarely / gets / .

→ _____

WORDS take a shower 샤워를 하다   surf the Internet 인터넷을 검색하다   at midnight 자정에
fast food 패스트푸드   crowded 붐비는   take a nap 낮잠을 자다   do the laundry 빨래를 하다
remember 기억하다

영작 술술

A 우리말과 같은 뜻이 되도록 빈칸에 알맞은 말을 쓰세요.

1 그녀는 보통 여가 시간에 피아노를 친다.

→ She ___usually___ ___plays___ the piano in her free time.

2 나는 널 보면 항상 기쁘다.

→ I _____ _____ happy to see you.

3 이곳은 겨울에 눈이 자주 내린다.

→ It _____ _____ here in the winter.

4 그는 자기 방을 거의 청소하지 않는다.

→ He _____ _____ his room.

5 그녀는 결코 노래하거나 춤추지 않는다.

→ She _____ _____ or dances.

6 Bob은 보통 방과 후에 한가하다.

→ Bob _____ _____ free after school.

7 너는 때때로 라디오를 듣니?

→ Do you _____ _____ to the radio?

8 나는 결코 다시는 늦지 않을 것이다.

→ I _____ _____ be late again.

9 아프리카는 항상 더운가요?

→ _____ it _____ hot in Africa?

10 나는 보통 저녁 식사 후에 산책을 간다.

→ I _____ _____ for a walk after dinner.

B 주어진 말을 이용하여 우리말을 영어로 바꿔 쓰세요.

1 우리 수학 선생님은 거의 웃지 않으신다. (smile)

➡ ___Our math teacher rarely smiles.___

2 나는 종종 내 우산을 잃어버린다. (lose, umbrella)

➡ _____

3 나는 그의 영어를 거의 이해하지 못한다. (understand, English)

➡ _____

4 그의 조언은 항상 도움이 된다. (advice, helpful)

➡ _____

5 Tony는 보통 자전거로 등교한다. (school, by bike)

➡ _____

6 너는 항상 안경을 쓰니? (wear glasses)

➡ _____

7 나는 결코 다시는 너를 보지 않을 거야. (will, see)

➡ _____

8 Kelly는 보통 저녁 식사를 거른다. (skip dinner)

➡ _____

9 너는 때때로 캠핑을 가니? (go camping)

➡ _____

10 그녀는 학교에 지각하는 일이 거의 없다. (late for school)

➡ _____

TIP 1

빈도부사는 일반동사 앞,
be동사나 조동사 뒤에
와요. 의문문에서는 주어
다음에 와요.

e.g.
- He always smiles.
- He is always happy.
- I will always love you.
- Is he always busy?

TIP 2

rarely와 never는 이미
부정의 의미가 포함되어
있기 때문에 부정어 not과
함께 쓸 수 없어요.

e.g.
- He doesn't rarely cry.
  (×)
- He rarely cries. (○)

WRAP UP

A Grammar 틀린 부분을 바르게 고쳐 문장을 다시 쓰세요.

1 I do always my homework. → __I always do my homework.__

2 Mary usually is friendly. → _____

3 He isn't rarely at the library. → _____

4 I won't never tell a lie. → _____

5 Harry wears sometimes a suit. → _____

6 John goes often to the gym. → _____

7 Do you see her always? → _____

B Writing 주어진 말을 이용하여 우리말을 영어로 바꿔 쓰세요.

1 그는 때때로 영화를 보러 간다. (go to the movies)

→ __He sometimes goes to the movies.__

2 나는 결코 그의 이름을 잊지 않을 것이다. (forget)

→ _____

3 그녀는 항상 여름에 선글라스를 쓴다. (wear sunglasses)

→ _____

4 George는 종종 방과 후에 축구를 한다. (soccer, after school)

→ _____

5 Lily는 거의 수업에 늦지 않는다. (be late for class)

→ _____

C 　내신 대비　질문을 읽고, 알맞은 답을 고르세요.

1 　다음 중 빈도부사의 위치가 <u>어색한</u> 것은?

　① I'll <u>never</u> give up.

　② She <u>always</u> is polite.

　③ Karen <u>usually</u> has lunch at 12.

　④ Do you <u>often</u> ride your bike?

2 　우리말을 영어로 바르게 옮긴 것은?

> 형과 나는 거의 함께 쇼핑하러 가지 않는다.

　① My brother and I rarely go shopping together.

　② My brother and I go rarely shopping together.

　③ My brother and I go shopping rarely together.

　④ My brother and I go shopping together rarely.

개념 Review

아래 빈칸을 채우면서 개념을 다시 한번 익혀보세요.

❶ 빈도부사의 종류

　☑ 빈도부사는 ❶ ＿＿＿＿＿＿＿ 를 나타내는 부사로 always(항상)부터 never(결코 ~않다)까지 다양한 종류가 있어요.

　☑ rarely와 never는 이미 부정의 의미를 포함하기 때문에 ❷ ＿＿＿＿＿＿＿ 과 함께 쓸 수 없어요.

❷ 빈도부사의 위치

　☑ 빈도부사는 일반동사 ❸ ＿＿＿＿＿ , be동사나 조동사 ❹ ＿＿＿＿＿ 에 위치해요.

　☑ 의문문에서는 빈도부사가 ❺ ＿＿＿＿＿ 뒤에 와요.

[01-02] 대화의 빈칸에 알맞은 말을 고르시오.

01

> A Congratulations. Your team won first prize.
> B Thank you. We worked very _____.

① hard

② hardly

③ high

④ highly

02

> A Do you walk to school, Jenny?
> B No, my dad _____ me to school.

① drive always

② always drive

③ drives always

④ always drives

03 다음 중 형용사와 부사가 잘못 짝지어진 것은?

① beautiful – beautifully

② quiet – quietly

③ lucky – luckily

④ fast – fastly

04 밑줄 친 단어의 쓰임이 다른 하나는?

① They left the party early.

② Ann always gets up early.

③ We had an early breakfast.

④ They came home early yesterday.

05 밑줄 친 부사의 쓰임이 어색한 것은?

① She entered the room quietly.

② They lived together happily.

③ He always speaks loudly.

④ The train arrived lately.

서술형

[06-07] 우리말과 같은 뜻이 되도록 빈칸에 알맞은 말을 쓰시오.

06

> 그는 그 상자를 쉽게 들어올렸다.

➡ He lifted the box _____.

07

> 저 새는 하늘 높이 날고 있다.

➡ The bird is flying _____ in the sky.

08 빈칸에 들어갈 말로 알맞은 것은?

> Her smile looks _____ today.

① sadly
② lovely
③ happily
④ seriously

09 빈칸에 들어갈 말로 알맞지 <u>않은</u> 것은?

> Paul drove his car _____.

① fastly
② safely
③ slowly
④ carefully

[10-11] 다음 중 <u>틀린</u> 문장을 고르시오.

10 ① You speak English very well.
② Finally, our exams are over.
③ I found the answer easily.
④ The boy jumped highly.

11 ① John never is on time.
② She rarely watches TV.
③ My brother is often sick.
④ I usually have dinner at 6.

[12-13] 우리말을 영어로 바르게 옮긴 것을 고르시오.

12
> 그는 훌륭한 배우이다. 그는 연기를 매우 잘한다.

① He is a great actor. He acts very good.
② He is a great actor. He acts very well.
③ He is a greatly actor. He acts very well.
④ He is a greatly actor. He acts very good.

13
> 그는 거의 우유를 마시지 않는다.

① He rarely drinks milk.
② He drinks rarely milk.
③ He rarely not drinks milk.
④ He doesn't rarely drink milk.

서술형

[14-15] <u>어색한</u> 부분을 바르게 고쳐 문장을 다시 쓰시오.

14
> Josh goes usually to school by bus.

➡ _____

15
> Is he late often for work?

➡ _____

06

의문사

학습목표

1   When, Where, Why 의문사의 의미와 의문문의 형태를 알아봐요.

2   Who, What 의문사의 의미와 의문문에서의 역할에 대해 알아봐요.

3   How 의문사의 의미와 「How+형용사/부사」의 다양한 의미를 알아봐요.

UNIT 01 When, Where, Why

1 의미

> Where are you from?

> I'm from France.

의문문		대답	
When is your birthday?	네 생일은 언제니?	It's on July 3.	7월 3일이야.
Where does she live?	그녀는 어디에 사니?	She lives in Seoul.	그녀는 서울에 살아.
Why are you late?	너는 왜 늦었니?	Because I missed my bus.	버스를 놓쳐서.

☑ 의문사 **when**(언제)은 때, **where**(어디서)는 장소, **why**(왜)는 이유를 물을 때 사용해요.

☑ 의문사가 쓰인 의문문은 Yes / No로 대답하지 않고 구체적으로 대답해요.

PRACTICE 1 When/Where/Why 넣기

❶ ____Where____ is your book? – It's in my bag.

❷ _____ is the party? – This Friday.

❸ _____ are you here? – Because I want to see you.

❹ _____ is he from? – He's from Spain.

2 의문문 만들기

> **Why** are you sad?

> Because I lost my cat.

의문문		
의문사+be동사	**When is** Susan's birthday? **Where are** Peter and Jane? **Why are** you running?	Susan의 생일은 언제니? Peter와 Jane은 어디에 있니? 너는 왜 뛰고 있니?
의문사+일반동사	**When do** you **eat** lunch? **Where does** George **live**? **Why did** she **cry** yesterday?	너는 언제 점심을 먹니? George는 어디에 사니? 그녀는 어제 왜 울었니?

☑ **be동사**가 있는 문장의 의문사 의문문은 「의문사＋be동사＋주어 ~?」의 형태예요.

☑ **일반동사**가 있는 문장의 의문사 의문문은 「의문사＋do / does / did＋주어＋동사원형 ~?」의 형태예요.

PRACTICE 2 알맞은 말 고르기

❶ When (is, does) the English test?

❷ Where (were, did) you at lunchtime?

❸ Why (was, did) he stay at home yesterday?

❹ When (is, does) the school festival start?

문법 쏙쏙

A 빈칸에 When, Where, Why 중에서 알맞은 의문사를 골라 쓰세요.

1 _____When_____ is your birthday? - It's on January 19.

2 _____ are my notebooks? - They are on the desk.

3 _____ is Rita so angry? - Because she lost her bag.

4 _____ is the field trip? - Next Friday.

5 _____ does the movie start? - At 7:30.

6 _____ do you eat lunch? - At the school cafeteria.

7 _____ are the children? - They are in the swimming pool.

8 _____ was John absent from class? – Because he was sick.

9 _____ did you first meet Henry? - Two years ago.

10 _____ is San Francisco? - It's in the United States.

11 _____ did they go last weekend? - They went to the zoo.

12 _____ is our school's anniversary? - On May 20.

13 _____ did you start playing tennis? - In 2020.

14 _____ did you open the window? - Because it was hot.

15 _____ did you buy that skirt? - I bought it at Macy's.

 WORDS January 1월   lose 잃어버리다   field trip 견학 여행, 현장 학습   cafeteria 구내식당, 카페테리아
absent 결석한   first 처음   May 5월   school's anniversary 개교기념일   skirt 치마

B 밑줄 친 부분을 묻는 의문문을 쓰세요.

1 Jack's birthday party is on Friday.
→ ___When is Jack's birthday party?___

2 My school is on Oak Street.
→ _____

3 Peggy is sad because her cat is sick.
→ _____

4 I get up at 7 o'clock every morning.
→ _____

5 He comes from China.
→ _____

6 They are going to the park.
→ _____

7 I visited my grandparents last week.
→ _____

8 I went to the dentist because I had a toothache.
→ _____

9 They went to the folk village yesterday.
→ _____

10 The driver stopped because he saw the red light.
→ _____

WORDS come from ~ 출신이다   have a toothache 이가 아프다   folk village 민속촌   driver 운전자
red light 빨간 신호등

A 우리말과 같은 뜻이 되도록 빈칸에 알맞은 말을 쓰세요.

1 우체국은 어디에 있나요?

➡ <u> Where </u> <u> is </u> the post office?

2 그녀의 결혼식은 언제입니까?

➡ _____ _____ her wedding?

3 그들은 왜 신나 있니?

➡ _____ _____ _____ excited?

4 너는 언제 태어났니?

➡ _____ _____ _____ born?

5 그녀는 왜 선글라스를 쓰고 있나요?

➡ _____ _____ she _____ sunglasses?

6 너의 아버지는 어디에서 일하시니?

➡ _____ _____ your father _____?

7 그 기차는 언제 도착했나요?

➡ _____ _____ the train _____?

8 너는 왜 어젯밤에 내게 전화했니?

➡ _____ _____ you _____ me last night?

9 너는 어디로 휴가를 갔니?

➡ _____ _____ you _____ for your vacation?

10 너는 저 새 책을 언제 샀니?

➡ _____ _____ you _____ that new book?

B 주어진 말을 이용하여 우리말을 영어로 바꿔 쓰세요.

1 네 휴대폰은 어디에 있니? (cellphone)

➡ _____Where is your cellphone?_____

2 수학 시험은 언제인가요? (the math test)

➡ _____

3 그 여자아이는 왜 울고 있나요? (cry)

➡ _____

4 그 아이들은 어디에서 놀고 있나요? (play)

➡ _____

5 Jenny는 왜 어제 늦었나요? (be late)

➡ _____

TIP 1

의문사 when은 때, where
는 장소, why는 이유를
물을 때 사용해요.

e.g.
- When is your birthday?
- Where is my cap?
- Why are you happy?

6 너는 언제 네 숙제를 끝냈니? (finish, homework)

➡ _____

7 너는 어디에서 자랐니? (grow up)

➡ _____

8 그녀는 왜 어제 공항에 갔나요? (the airport)

➡ _____

TIP 2

be동사가 있는 의문사
의문문은 「의문사+be동사
+주어 ~?」이고,
일반동사가 있는 의문사
의문문은 「의문사+
do/does/did+주어+
동사원형 ~?」의 형태예요.

e.g.
- Where is he?
- Where are you going?
- Where does he live?

9 너는 저 원피스를 어디에서 샀니? (that dress)

➡ _____

10 당신은 언제 그 이메일을 보냈나요? (send, email)

➡ _____

WRAP UP

A Grammar 틀린 부분을 바르게 고쳐 문장을 다시 쓰세요.

1 Where City Hall is? → _Where is City Hall?_

2 When you met him? → _____

3 Where is your birthday? → _____

4 Where they did go? → _____

5 Why you are so happy? → _____

6 Where is him? → _____

7 Why you bought that book? → _____

B Writing 주어진 말을 이용하여 우리말을 영어로 바꿔 쓰세요.

1 약국은 어디에 있나요? (the drugstore)

→ _Where is the drugstore?_

2 은행들은 언제 문을 여나요? (the banks)

→ _____

3 너는 그것을 어디에서 찾았니? (find)

→ _____

4 당신은 언제부터 여기서 일하기 시작했나요? (start working)

→ _____

5 그는 왜 Julie를 만났니? (meet)

→ _____

C [내신 대비] 질문을 읽고, 알맞은 답을 고르세요.

1 다음 중 문장이 <u>틀린</u> 것은?

① When is her concert?

② Why she is always busy?

③ Why did Jack quit his job?

④ Where did you see Mark?

2 우리말을 영어로 바르게 옮긴 것은?

> 너는 어디서 친구들을 만났니?

① Where you meet your friends?

② Where did you meet your friends?

③ Where do you meet your friends?

④ Where are you meeting your friends?

개념 Review

아래 빈칸을 채우면서 개념을 다시 한번 익혀보세요.

① 의문사의 의미: When, Where, Why

☑ 의문사 **①** _____ (언제)은 때, **②** _____ (어디서)는 장소, **③** _____ (왜)는 이유를 물을 때 사용해요.

☑ 의문사가 쓰인 의문문은 **④** _____ 로 대답하지 않고 구체적으로 대답해요.

② 의문문 만들기: When, Where, Why

☑ **⑤** _____ 가 있는 문장의 의문사 의문문은 「의문사 + be동사 + 주어 ~?」의 형태예요.

☑ **⑥** _____ 가 있는 문장의 의문사 의문문은 「의문사 + do / does / did + 주어 + 동사원형 ~?」의 형태예요.

UNIT 02 Who, What

1 의미

What are you doing?

I'm doing my homework.

의문문		대답	
Who is he?	그는 누구니?	He is my brother.	그는 내 남동생이야.
Who is in the kitchen?	주방에 누가 있니?	Jane is there.	Jane이 그곳에 있어.
What is this?	이것은 무엇이니?	It's a pencil case.	그것은 필통이야.
What did Andy buy?	Andy는 무엇을 샀니?	He bought a T-shirt.	그는 티셔츠를 샀어.
What color do you like?	너는 무슨 색을 좋아해?	I like orange.	나는 주황색을 좋아해.

☑ 의문사 **who**(누구)는 사람에 대해, **what**(무엇)은 사물에 대해 물을 때 사용해요.

☑ 의문사 what 뒤에 **명사**가 오면 '**무슨(어떤) ~**'라고 해석해요.

PRACTICE 1 알맞은 의문사 고르기

❶ (Who, What) is that man over there?

❷ (Who, What) is your teacher's name?

❸ (Who, What) food do you like?

❹ (Who, What) is your favorite singer?

2 의문문 만들기

의문사의 역할	의문문	대답
의문사가 목적어인 경우	**Who** did you meet? 너는 누구를 만났니? **What** does John sell? John은 무엇을 파니?	I met *Sarah*. 나는 Sarah를 만났어. John sells *furniture*. John은 가구를 팔아.
의문사가 주어인 경우	**Who** helped her? 누가 그녀를 도왔니? **What** happened? 무슨 일이 일어났니?	*Frank* helped her. Frank가 그녀를 도왔어. *An accident* happened. 사고가 발생했어.

☑ 의문사 who와 what은 문장의 **목적어**와 **주어**를 대신해 쓰일 수 있어요.

☑ who와 what이 주어인 경우에는 바로 뒤에 동사가 와서 「의문사＋동사 ～?」의 어순이 돼요.
e.g. Who *did help* her? (X)　　Who *helped* her? (O)

PRACTICE **2**　**Who/What 넣기**

❶ Mike won the race.　　→ ___Who___ won the race?

❷ Tom broke <u>my glasses</u>.　　→ _____ did Tom break?

❸ Romeo loves <u>Juliet</u>.　　→ _____ does Romeo love?

❹ <u>The frame</u> fell off the wall.　　→ _____ fell off the wall?

A ( ) 안에서 알맞은 의문사를 고르세요.

1 ((Who), What) is that man with the black hat?

2 (Who, What) do you eat for breakfast?

3 (Who, What) did Sarah meet yesterday?

4 (Who, What) color is your shirt?

5 (Who, What) invented the computer?

6 (Who, What) is in the briefcase?

7 (Who, What) ate all the chocolate cake?

8 (Who, What) is your favorite subject?

9 (Who, What) is the best student in your class?

10 (Who, What) is the name of the mountain?

11 (Who, What) asked the question?

12 (Who, What) sport does he play?

13 (Who, What) won the lottery?

14 (Who, What) is Bob doing right now?

15 (Who, What) is Jane talking to?

 WORDS **invent** 발명하다　**briefcase** 서류 가방　**subject** 과목　**win the lottery** 복권에 당첨되다　**talk to** ~와 이야기하다

B 다음 밑줄 친 부분을 묻는 의문문을 쓰세요.

1 My brother's name is Mike.

   ➡ What is your brother's name?

2 My uncle designed the house.

   ➡ _____

3 Jack saw Karen at the park.

   ➡ _____

4 The boys are playing hide and seek.

   ➡ _____

5 Sally invited Nick to dinner.

   ➡ _____

6 I visited my aunt last weekend.

   ➡ _____

7 I had a sandwich and some milk for lunch.

   ➡ _____

8 The light fell off the ceiling.

   ➡ _____

9 She dropped her handkerchief.

   ➡ _____

10 The teacher is grading the tests.

   ➡ _____

WORDS design 디자인[설계]하다 play hide and seek 숨바꼭질하다 invite someone to dinner ~를 저녁 식사에 초대하다 light 전등 fall off ~에서 떨어지다 ceiling 천장 drop 떨어뜨리다 handkerchief 손수건 grade 채점하다

A 우리말과 같은 뜻이 되도록 빈칸에 알맞은 말을 쓰세요.

1 네가 가장 좋아하는 선생님은 누구니?

➡ ___Who___ ___is___ your favorite teacher?

2 네 가방에는 무엇이 들어있니?

➡ _____ _____ in your bag?

3 누가 그 상자들을 옮겼나요?

➡ _____ _____ the boxes?

4 그는 무엇을 읽고 있나요?

➡ _____ _____ he _____?

5 당신에게 무슨 일이 일어났나요?

➡ _____ _____ to you?

6 너는 누구와 이야기하고 싶니?

➡ _____ _____ you want to talk to?

7 너는 어제 누구를 만났니?

➡ _____ _____ you _____ yesterday?

8 누가 설거지를 할 건가요?

➡ _____ _____ _____ _____ do the dishes?

9 너는 어제 무슨 영화를 봤니?

➡ _____ _____ _____ you watch yesterday?

10 너는 지난 주말에 무엇을 샀니?

➡ _____ _____ you _____ last weekend?

B 주어진 말을 이용하여 우리말을 영어로 바꿔 쓰세요.

1 저 여자아이는 누구니? (that girl)

➡   Who is that girl?

2 네가 좋아하는 TV 프로그램은 무엇이니? (favorite, TV show)

➡

3 그 서랍 안에는 무엇이 들어있나요? (the drawer)

➡

4 누가 이 방을 청소했나요? (clean this room)

➡

5 Sam은 누구를 좋아하니? (like)

➡

6 너는 주말에 주로 무엇을 하니? (usually, on the weekend)

➡

7 그녀는 무엇을 요리하고 있나요? (cook)

➡

8 너는 수업 시간에 무엇을 질문했니? (ask, during class)

➡

9 당신은 저녁 식사에 누구를 초대했나요? (to dinner)

➡

10 너는 어떤 책을 읽고 있니? (read)

➡

TIP 1

의문사 who(누구)는 사람, what(무엇)은 사물에 대해 물을 때 사용해요. what 뒤에 명사가 오면 '무슨(어떤) ~'라고 해석해요.

e.g.
- Who is she?
- What is this?
- What food do you like?

TIP 2

의문사 who와 what이 주어인 경우에는 의문문 어순을 따르지 않고 「의문사+동사 ~?」 형태로 만들어요.

e.g.
- A book is on the table.
  → What is on the table?
- Ann saw Jack.
  → Who saw Jack?

WRAP UP

A Grammar 틀린 부분을 바르게 고쳐 문장을 다시 쓰세요.

1 Who Andrew is? ➡ Who is Andrew?

2 What you are doing? ➡ _____

3 Who is his address? ➡ _____

4 Who did win the prize? ➡ _____

5 What you did last weekend? ➡ _____

6 Who did make this pasta? ➡ _____

7 What did happened last night? ➡ _____

B Writing 주어진 말을 이용하여 우리말을 영어로 바꿔 쓰세요.

1 그들은 누구입니까? (they)

  ➡ Who are they?

2 네가 좋아하는 음식은 무엇이니? (favorite)

  ➡ _____

3 너는 어떤 게임을 했니? (game, play)

  ➡ _____

4 누가 시험에 떨어졌습니까? (fail the exam)

  ➡ _____

5 너는 방과 후에 주로 무엇을 하니? (usually, after school)

  ➡ _____

C [내신 대비] 질문을 읽고, 알맞은 답을 고르세요.

1 Who와 What 중에서 빈칸에 들어갈 말이 <u>다른</u> 하나는?

① _____ is he eating?

② _____ saw the accident?

③ _____ did they do there?

④ _____ is your phone number?

2 우리말을 영어로 바르게 옮긴 것은?

> 누가 저 문을 열었습니까?

① Who opened that door?

② Who did open that door?

③ Who was open that door?

④ Who did you open that door?

개념 Review

아래 빈칸을 채우면서 개념을 다시 한번 익혀보세요.

❶ **의문사의 의미: Who, What**

☑ 의문사 **❶** _____ (누구)는 사람에 대해, **❷** _____ (무엇)은 사물에 대해 물을 때 사용해요.

☑ 의문사 what 뒤에 **❸** _____ 가 오면 '무슨(어떤) ~'라고 해석해요.

❷ **의문사의 역할: Who, What**

☑ 의문사 who와 what은 문장의 목적어와 **❹** _____ 를 대신해 쓰일 수 있어요.

☑ who와 what이 주어인 경우에는 바로 뒤에 동사가 와서 「의문사＋동사 ~?」의 어순이 돼요.

UNIT 03 How

1 의미

How is the weather there?

It's very nice.

의문문		대답	
How are you?	어떻게 지내?	Great.	아주 잘 지내.
How was your trip?	여행은 어땠어?	It was fantastic.	아주 좋았어.
How did he fix it?	그는 어떻게 그것을 고쳤니?	He called a repairman.	그는 수리공을 불렀어.
How do you go to work?	너는 어떻게 회사에 가니?	By bus.	버스로 가.

☑ 의문사 **how**는 '**어떤, 어떻게**'라는 의미로 주로 상태, 방법, 수단 등을 물을 때 사용해요.

PRACTICE 1 질문/대답 연결하기

❶ How is your brother? •   • It was terrible.

❷ How was your date? •   • I walked.

❸ How did they play? •   • He's good.

❹ How did you get there? •   • They played very well.

2 How+형용사/부사

> How tall are you?

> I'm 158 centimeters tall.

How+형용사/부사			
How old	몇 살인, 얼마나 오래된	**How old** are you?	너는 몇 살이니?
How tall	(키, 높이가) 얼마나 큰	**How tall** is he?	그는 키가 얼마나 크니?
How big	(크기가) 얼마나 큰	**How big** is the house?	그 집은 얼마나 크니?
How long	얼마나 긴/오랫동안	**How long** is the river?	그 강은 얼마나 기니?
How far	얼마나 먼	**How far** is the restaurant?	그 식당은 얼마나 머니?
How often	얼마나 자주	**How often** do you exercise?	너는 얼마나 자주 운동하니?
How well	얼마나 잘	**How well** do you know him?	너는 그를 얼마나 잘 아니?

☑ 의문사 how 뒤에 **형용사**나 **부사**가 오면 다양한 의미가 될 수 있어요. 이때 how는 '**얼마나**'로 해석해요.

PRACTICE 2 알맞은 형용사/부사 넣기

big	often	tall	well

❶ How _____tall_____ is that tower?

❷ How _____ is the jumbo pizza?

❸ How _____ does she speak English?

❹ How _____ do you go to the movies?

문법 쏙쏙

A 밑줄 친 부분을 묻는 의문문을 쓰세요.

1 I am <u>fine</u> today.
→ How are you today?

2 The coffee is <u>very bitter</u>.
→

3 The weather in Alaska is <u>very cold</u>.
→

4 Jane dances <u>very gracefully</u>.
→

5 She looks <u>lovely</u> in that dress.
→

6 Jack and Peggy go to school <u>by bus</u>.
→

7 The basketball player is <u>192 centimeters tall</u>.
→

8 The temple is <u>one hundred years old</u>.
→

9 I studied <u>for five hours</u> last night.
→

10 My mom does grocery shopping <u>once a week</u>.
→

WORDS gracefully 우아하게   temple 절, 사원   hundred 백, 100   do grocery shopping 장을 보다
once a week 일주일에 한 번

B 주어진 말을 바르게 배열하여 문장을 완성하세요.

1 are / feeling / you / how / today / ?
→   How are you feeling today?

2 to Japan / how / your trip / was / ?
→ _____

3 Carol / did / sing / how / ?
→ _____

4 the problem / they / how / solve / did / ?
→ _____

5 go / does / how / to work / Mary / ?
→ _____

6 how / you / in Europe / travel / did / ?
→ _____

7 how / the new shopping mall / is / big / ?
→ _____

8 old / your brother / is / how / ?
→ _____

9 far / the hospital / how / is / from here / ?
→ _____

10 have / often / do / P.E. class / how / you / ?
→ _____

WORDS   travel 여행하다   hospital 병원   P.E. class 체육 수업

영작 술술

A 우리말과 같은 뜻이 되도록 빈칸에 알맞은 말을 쓰세요.

1 너의 부모님은 어떻게 지내시니?

➡ ___How___ ___are___ your parents?

2 태국 여행은 어땠니?

➡ _____ _____ your trip to Thailand?

3 제가 이 원피스 입은 거 어때 보여요?

➡ _____ _____ _____ look in this dress?

4 그는 회사에 어떻게 가나요?

➡ _____ _____ _____ go to work?

5 너는 그 손목시계를 어떻게 찾았니?

➡ _____ _____ _____ find the watch?

6 역은 여기서 얼마나 멉니까?

➡ _____ _____ _____ the station from here?

7 네 아버지는 키가 얼마나 크니?

➡ _____ _____ _____ your father?

8 그는 뉴욕에 얼마나 오랫동안 머물렀나요?

➡ _____ _____ _____ he stay in New York?

9 한국에는 얼마나 자주 눈이 내립니까?

➡ _____ _____ _____ it snow in Korea?

10 그녀는 얼마나 잘 노래를 불렀나요?

➡ _____ _____ _____ she sing?

B 주어진 말을 이용하여 우리말을 영어로 바꿔 쓰세요.

1 오늘 날씨가 어때요? (the weather)

➡   How is the weather today?

2 네 여름 방학은 어땠어? (summer vacation)

➡ _____

3 Michael은 학교에 어떻게 가나요? (go to school)

➡ _____

4 너는 네 남자친구를 어떻게 처음 만났니? (first meet)

➡ _____

5 그 연못은 얼마나 큽니까? (the pond)

➡ _____

6 경복궁은 얼마나 오래되었습니까? (Gyeongbok Palace)

➡ _____

7 주유소는 여기서 얼마나 먼가요? (the gas station)

➡ _____

8 너는 얼마나 자주 외식을 하니? (eat out)

➡ _____

9 그들은 경기를 얼마나 잘했나요? (play)

➡ _____

10 그는 캐나다에서 얼마나 오래 살았습니까? (live in Canada)

➡ _____

TIP 1

'어떻게 지내요?'라고 인사할 때는 다음과 같이 말할 수 있어요.

e.g.
- How are you?
- How are you doing?
- How is it going?
- How is everything?

TIP 2

How는 형용사나 부사와 함께 쓰여 다양한 의문문을 만들 수 있어요.

e.g.
- How old are you?
- How tall is he?
- How often do you exercise?

WRAP UP

A Grammar 대화가 완성되도록 빈칸에 알맞은 말을 쓰세요.

1 _____How_____ _____was_____ the show? – It was great.

2 _____ _____ he drive? – He drives very fast.

3 _____ _____ you make pizza? – I found a recipe on the Internet.

4 _____ _____ he go to work every day? – By subway.

5 _____ _____ is Brian? – He is 178 centimeters tall.

6 _____ _____ is the subway station? – It's 2 kilometers from here.

7 _____ _____ do you take taxis? – About twice a month.

B Writing 주어진 말을 이용하여 우리말을 영어로 바꿔 쓰세요.

1 그 영화는 어땠나요? (movie)

   ➡ How was the movie?

2 시청은 어떻게 가나요? (get to City Hall)

   ➡ _____

3 네 개는 얼마나 크니? (big)

   ➡ _____

4 그는 일을 얼마나 잘합니까? (well, work)

   ➡ _____

5 너는 얼마나 자주 머리를 자르니? (get a haircut)

   ➡ _____

C [내신 대비] 질문을 읽고, 알맞은 답을 고르세요.

1 빈칸에 들어갈 의문사가 <u>다른</u> 하나는?

① _____ is your teacher?

② _____ did you get there?

③ _____ is your favorite color?

④ _____ old is your grandfather?

2 우리말을 영어로 바르게 옮긴 것은?

> 당신은 얼마나 자주 쇼핑을 가나요?

① How often you go shopping?

② How do you often go shopping?

③ How do you go shopping often?

④ How often do you go shopping?

개념 Review

아래 빈칸을 채우면서 개념을 다시 한번 익혀보세요.

❶ 의문사의 의미: how

☑ 의문사 how는 '❶ _____ '라는 의미로 주로 상태, 방법, 수단 등을 물을 때 사용해요.

❷ How + 형용사 / 부사

☑ 의문사 how 뒤에 ❷ _____ 나 ❸ _____ 가 오면 다양한 의미가 될 수 있어요. 이때
how는 '❹ _____ '로 해석해요.

[01-03] 대화의 빈칸에 알맞은 말을 고르시오.

01

> A _____ does the library close?
> B On Sundays.

① Why
② How
③ When
④ Where

02

> A _____ are they doing?
> B They are solving a puzzle.

① Who
② What
③ Where
④ How

03

> A _____ bought this book?
> B I did. Do you want to read it?

① Where
② When
③ Who
④ Why

04 빈칸에 공통으로 들어갈 말로 알맞은 것은?

> • _____ is your brother?
> • _____ long is your holiday?

① Who
② Where
③ What
④ How

05 질문에 대한 대답으로 알맞은 것은?

> How did you go to Busan?

① In 2010.
② By plane.
③ For 15 days.
④ It was great.

서술형

[06-07] 빈칸에 알맞은 말을 써넣어 대화를 완성하시오.

06

> A _____ did you meet at the party?
> B I met Jack and Sandy.

07

> A _____ _____ is the subway station?
> B It's 1.5 kilometers from here.

08 다음 중 대화가 <u>어색한</u> 것은?

① A: How are you?
   B: I'm great. Thank you.

② A: Where is she from?
   B: She's from Canada.

③ A: When do you play tennis?
   B: Once a month.

④ A: Why is he running?
   B: Because he is in a hurry.

09 다음 중 밑줄 친 부분이 <u>틀린</u> 것은?

① <u>How old</u> is the castle?

② <u>How well</u> does she cook?

③ <u>How long</u> is that building?

④ <u>How often</u> do you read books?

서술형

[10-11] 밑줄 친 부분을 알맞은 의문사로 고쳐 쓰시오.

10
> <u>What</u> did you go on your last vacation?

→ _____

11
> <u>How</u> color are you going to paint the door?

→ _____

12 빈칸에 들어갈 수 <u>없는</u> 의문사는?

> _____ did you go to the shop?

① When

② Who

③ Why

④ How

13 우리말을 영어로 바르게 옮긴 것은?

> 누가 내 샌드위치를 먹었니?

① Who ate my sandwich?

② Who did ate my sandwich?

③ Who did eat my sandwich?

④ Who did you eat my sandwich?

서술형

[14-15] 주어진 말을 바르게 배열하여 문장을 완성하시오.

14
> like / subject / do / you / what

→ _____ ?

15
> he / drive / often / to work / how / does

→ _____ ?

Grammar Plus Writing

START

WORKBOOK

2

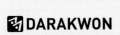 DARAKWON

Grammar +Plus Writing

START

WORKBOOK 2

셀 수 있는 명사

A 밑줄 친 부분이 맞으면 O를 쓰고, <u>틀리면</u> 바르게 고치세요.

1 Do you have <u>an orange</u>? ➔ _____

2 She traveled to many <u>country</u>. ➔ _____

3 He saw two <u>mouse</u> in the house. ➔ _____

4 Ants have six <u>leg</u>. ➔ _____

5 Mary has two movie <u>tickets</u>. ➔ _____

6 He gave me <u>a umbrella</u>. ➔ _____

7 My dad caught five <u>fishes</u>. ➔ _____

8 She bought a peach and two <u>tomatos</u>. ➔ _____

9 The three <u>man</u> are from England. ➔ _____

10 Mom is wearing <u>a blue scarf</u>. ➔ _____

11 A <u>children</u> is walking a dog. ➔ _____

12 Two <u>cats</u> are sleeping on the sofa. ➔ _____

13 Look at the four <u>sheeps</u> over there! ➔ _____

14 I can't find my <u>glasses</u>. ➔ _____

15 My brother likes to play with <u>toys</u>. ➔ _____

Answer Key p.22

B 주어진 말을 이용하여 우리말을 영어로 바꿔 쓰세요.

1 그 해변들은 부드러운 모래가 있다. (have, soft sand)

➡ _____

2 내 여동생은 분홍색 원피스를 좋아한다. (love, dress)

➡ _____

3 나의 가족은 이번 여름에 한 섬을 방문했다. (island, this summer)

➡ _____

4 자기 전에 네 이를 닦아라. (brush, before bed)

➡ _____

5 내 이웃들은 친절하고 멋지다. (kind, nice)

➡ _____

6 그 아기의 발은 아주 작고 귀엽다. (baby's, so, small, cute)

➡ _____

7 Mike는 접시 몇 개를 깨뜨렸다. (break, a few, dish)

➡ _____

8 나뭇잎들은 가을에 색들을 바꾼다. (change, color, in fall)

➡ _____

9 도시들은 많은 사람들과 건물들을 가지고 있다. (many, building)

➡ _____

10 Kate는 상자들 속에 그 옷들을 넣었다. (put, clothes)

➡ _____

A ( ) 안에서 알맞은 것을 고르세요.

1   Andrew drinks (a milk, milk) every morning.

2   I cleaned my new (furniture, furnitures).

3   Put (a bowl of, a slice of) cheese on the bread.

4   We need some (meat, meats) for the stew.

5   Good (luck, lucks) on your test!

6   We bought three (bar, bars) of soap.

7   She planted some (flower, flowers) in the garden.

8   Jessie ordered (a bowl of, a piece of) onion soup.

9   We can find (beauty, beauties) in nature.

10   Listen to your parents' (advice, advices).

11   My grandmother baked two (loafs, loaves) of bread.

12   Could you give me a cup of (water, waters)?

13   Add some (salt, salts) to the fried egg.

14   Let's hurry. We don't have enough (times, time).

15   He ate (a piece of, a cup of) cheesecake.

Answer Key p.22

B 주어진 말을 바르게 배열하여 문장을 완성하세요.

1 이탈리아는 음식으로 유명하다. (famous, Italy, is, for food)

➡ _____

2 내 친구가 내게 사탕 한 상자를 주었다. (candy, my friend, me, a box of, gave)

➡ _____

3 토요일은 내가 가장 좋아하는 날이다. (my, Saturday, day, is, favorite)

➡ _____

4 그 푸딩에는 많은 설탕이 있다. (sugar, the pudding, a lot of, has)

➡ _____

5 Ted는 망고 주스 한 병을 마셨다. (mango juice, Ted, a bottle of, drank)

➡ _____

6 그녀는 새 신발을 위해 돈을 좀 모았다. (some, she, saved, new shoes, money, for)

➡ _____

7 나는 디저트로 초콜릿 바 한 개를 먹었다. (ate, a bar of, I, for dessert, chocolate)

➡ _____

8 너는 댄스 음악을 듣는 것을 좋아하니? (do, like to, dance music, you, listen to)

➡ _____

9 그는 힘든 일로 피곤했다. (he, hard, from, work, tired, was)

➡ _____

10 그 웨이터는 물 두 잔을 가져다 주었다. (two, the waiter, of water, brought, glasses)

➡ _____

인칭대명사

A 밑줄 친 부분을 바르게 고치세요.

1 <u>Them</u> are from Germany. ➡ _____

2 That isn't my bag. <u>My</u> is red. ➡ _____

3 Our neighbor is very kind. We love <u>she</u>. ➡ _____

4 Did you see Josh and <u>him</u> sister? ➡ _____

5 The blue bike is <u>our</u>. ➡ _____

6 I love dolls and collect <u>it</u>. ➡ _____

7 Is the man <u>you</u> English teacher? ➡ _____

8 Eric and <u>me</u> went to the movies. ➡ _____

9 The bird built <u>it</u> nest in the tree. ➡ _____

10 My hat is here. <u>Your</u> is there. ➡ _____

11 Do you know <u>his</u>? He is a famous actor. ➡ _____

12 <u>Ours</u> pizza just arrived. ➡ _____

13 She invited <u>we</u> to her house. ➡ _____

14 My dad likes old things. They are <u>him</u>. ➡ _____

15 We shared our snacks. They shared <u>their</u>, too. ➡ _____

Answer Key p.22

B 주어진 말을 이용하여 우리말을 영어로 바꿔 쓰세요.

1 나는 그녀의 얼굴을 기억하지 못한다. (not, remember, face)

➡ _____

2 그 안경은 그녀의 것이니? (glasses)

➡ _____

3 너는 그와 함께 수영하러 갈 거니? (will, go swimming, with)

➡ _____

4 Erin은 내 프로젝트를 하는 데 나를 도와주었다. (help, with, project)

➡ _____

5 그 귀여운 토끼들은 그의 것이다. (cute rabbit)

➡ _____

6 네 것은 책상 위에 있니? (is, the desk)

➡ _____

7 그 가족은 그들의 개를 산책시키는 것을 좋아한다. (like, walk one's dog)

➡ _____

8 모든 사람들이 그의 아이디어를 좋아한다. (everyone, likes)

➡ _____

9 우리는 그들과 함께 축구를 했다. (play soccer, with)

➡ _____

10 우리 선생님은 우리에게 흥미로운 이야기를 읽어 주신다. (read, interesting stories)

➡ _____

지시대명사

A ( ) 안에서 알맞은 것을 고르세요.

1 (This, These) is my new jacket.

2 Is (that, those) your cap?

3 We like (this, these) chocolate cookies.

4 Mom, (this, these) is my friend Andrew.

5 Look at those (bird, birds) in the sky!

6 (This, These) lake is very deep.

7 Can you pass me (that, those) book?

8 Are (this, these) your sneakers?

9 (That, Those) erasers are mine.

10 Eric gave me (this, these) scissors.

11 (That is, Those are) our favorite games.

12 (That, Those) is his new house.

13 Did you take (that, those) pictures?

14 Try (this, these) dessert for free.

15 (This, These) are the gifts for my grandmother.

Answer Key p.22

B 우리말을 참고하여 밑줄 친 부분을 바르게 고쳐 문장을 다시 쓰세요.

1 <u>Is this</u> your socks?   이것은 네 양말이니?

→ _____

2 <u>That is</u> my cousin Sam.   이 사람은 내 사촌 Sam이야.

→ _____

3 <u>Those are</u> a famous tower.   저것은 유명한 탑이다.

→ _____

4 I borrowed <u>these</u> book from Jake.   나는 Jake에게 이 책을 빌렸다.

→ _____

5 She made <u>this beautiful painting</u>.   그녀는 이 아름다운 그림들을 만들었다.

→ _____

6 My dad climbs <u>this</u> mountain.   나의 아빠는 저 산을 등산한다.

→ _____

7 Pour <u>those oil</u> into the pan.   팬에 저 기름을 부어라.

→ _____

8 <u>Those musician</u> played music together.   저 음악가들은 함께 음악을 연주했다.

→ _____

9 <u>Is these</u> your family photos?   이것들은 네 가족사진이니?

→ _____

10 <u>These are</u> my sister's dresses.   저것들은 내 여동생의 원피스이다.

→ _____

There is / are

A ( ) 안에서 알맞은 것을 고르세요.

1 There (is, are) a tall tree near my house.

2 There (is, are) some children on the playground.

3 There (isn't, aren't) any juice in the bottle.

4 (Is, Are) there any earphones on the bed?

5 There (isn't, aren't) any cars on the road.

6 There (is, are) a lot of stores on the street.

7 (Is, Are) there any meat in the refrigerator?

8 There (isn't, aren't) a hospital near here.

9 There (is, are) two cups of coffee on the table.

10 (Is, Are) there a swimming pool at the hotel?

11 There (isn't, aren't) any mistakes in her essay.

12 There (is, are) too much sugar in the juice.

13 There (is, are) three libraries in my town.

14 (Is, Are) there many people in the park?

15 There (isn't, aren't) many buses to the museum.

Answer Key p.23

B 주어진 말을 이용하여 우리말을 영어로 바꿔 쓰세요.

1 나무에 원숭이 몇 마리가 있다. (some, monkey, in the tree)

➡ _____

2 그 도시에 큰 호수 하나가 있다. (big lake, in the city)

➡ _____

3 길을 따라 많은 카페들이 있다. (many, café, along the street)

➡ _____

4 이 근처에 은행이 있나요? (a bank)

➡ _____

5 하늘에 별이 많지 않다. (not, many, in the sky)

➡ _____

6 화장실에 비누가 조금도 없다. (any, soap, in the bathroom)

➡ _____

7 일 년에 12달이 있다. (month, in a year)

➡ _____

8 선반 위에 빵이 많이 있다. (a lot of, on the shelf)

➡ _____

9 경기장에 축구 선수들이 있습니까? (soccer player, on the field)

➡ _____

10 로마에는 새 건물이 많이 있지 않다. (many, new building, in Rome)

➡ _____

A 빈칸에 it과 there 중에서 알맞은 말을 골라 쓰세요.

1 Is _____ cold out there?

2 _____ is already 12:30.

3 Is _____ a bus stop near here?

4 _____ was my dad's birthday yesterday.

5 _____ is fall, but it is still hot.

6 _____ is far from here to the mall.

7 _____ is a policeman on the road.

8 Is _____ Thursday or Friday today?

9 In Sokcho, _____ snows a lot in winter.

10 Is _____ 6 o'clock now?

11 _____ is a big park next to the station.

12 _____ is a 5-minute walk to the library.

13 _____ was a beautiful day today.

14 _____ is October 31 today. It's Halloween.

15 _____ was no rain yesterday.

Answer Key p.23

B 주어진 말과 it을 이용하여 우리말을 영어로 바꿔 쓰세요.

1 오늘은 덥고 화창했다. (hot, sunny today)

➡ _____

2 지금 뉴욕은 9시인가요? (o'clock, New York now)

➡ _____

3 바쁜 주말이었다. (a busy weekend)

➡ _____

4 내일 바람이 많이 불 것이다. (be going to, windy tomorrow)

➡ _____

5 오늘이 Sue의 생일입니까? (birthday today)

➡ _____

6 우리 집에서 공원까지 멀지 않다. (far, from, to, park)

➡ _____

7 시드니는 지금 여름이다. (summer, Sydney, now)

➡ _____

8 어제가 6월 1일이었나요? (June 1 yesterday)

➡ _____

9 여기는 비가 많이 내리고 있다. (rain, a lot here)

➡ _____

10 사무실까지 운전으로 30분 거리이다. (30-minute drive, the office)

➡ _____

A 주어진 형용사가 들어갈 위치로 알맞은 곳에 V표 하세요.

1 His car is and broken. (old)

2 We had a weekend. (nice)

3 Lemons taste too. (sour)

4 The movie is not. (funny)

5 She is a singer in Korea. (famous)

6 The fog is today. (thick)

7 Her baby looks lovely and. (cute)

8 Emily felt after the hard work. (tired)

9 I bought a T-shirt online. (cheap)

10 The flowers smell. (sweet)

11 Daniel has hair. (short)

12 My grandmother made me cookies. (delicious)

13 Don't do that. It's. (dangerous)

14 There is a house near here. (small)

15 It is in winter in Alaska. (cold)

B 주어진 말을 바르게 배열하여 문장을 완성하세요.

1 그 오래된 집은 무서워 보인다. (the, scary, old, looks, house)

➡ _____

2 신선한 채소들은 건강하다. (fresh, are, vegetables, healthy)

➡ _____

3 Josh는 영리한 학생이다. (clever, Josh, a, student, is)

➡ _____

4 네 생각이 훌륭하게 들린다. (great, your, sounds, idea)

➡ _____

5 우리는 훌륭한 저녁 식사를 했다. (we, wonderful, a, had, dinner)

➡ _____

6 교통이 오늘 혼잡하다. (traffic, heavy today, the, is)

➡ _____

7 나는 집에서 편안함을 느낀다. (feel, at home, I, comfortable)

➡ _____

8 저기에 긴 다리가 있다. (long, is, over there, bridge, a, there)

➡ _____

9 그 롤러코스터는 매우 빠르다. (the, fast, roller coaster, very, is)

➡ _____

10 Brown 씨는 형형색색의 넥타이를 가지고 있다. (has, Mr. Brown, neckties, colorful)

➡ _____

A 밑줄 친 부분이 맞으면 O를 쓰고, <u>틀리면</u> 바르게 고치세요.

1 There are <u>much</u> trees in the park. → _____

2 Put <u>some</u> salt on the pasta. → _____

3 We didn't eat <u>any</u> food yet. → _____

4 Do you get <u>many</u> snow in the winter? → _____

5 My friends gave me <u>much</u> gifts. → _____

6 <u>Some people</u> love to travel. → _____

7 He doesn't have <u>many</u> furniture in his house. → _____

8 I borrowed some <u>book</u> from Andy. → _____

9 Do you need <u>any help</u> with your work? → _____

10 I watched <u>any</u> movies last weekend. → _____

11 Can you give me <u>any</u> ideas? → _____

12 There isn't <u>many</u> ice cream in the refrigerator. → _____

13 I don't have <u>some</u> water in my bottle. → _____

14 She drinks <u>a lot of</u> coffee every day. → _____

15 Are there <u>much</u> people in the restaurant? → _____

Answer Key p.24

B 주어진 말을 바르게 배열하여 문장을 완성하세요.

1 파리에 많은 관광객들이 있다. (tourists, in Paris, there, many, are)

➡ _____

2 이번 여름에 비가 많이 내렸다. (a lot of, got, rain, this summer, we)

➡ _____

3 접시에 빵이 조금도 없다. (any, isn't, on, bread, the plate, there)

➡ _____

4 나는 하늘에 아름다운 구름을 좀 봤다. (some, clouds, I, beautiful, saw, in the sky)

➡ _____

5 당신은 질문이 좀 있습니까? (you, any, do, questions, have)

➡ _____

6 많은 아이들이 게임하는 것을 즐긴다. (playing, a lot of, enjoy, children, games)

➡ _____

7 나는 과일과 계란이 좀 필요하다. (I, and, need, fruit, some, eggs)

➡ _____

8 나의 이웃은 많은 소음을 낸다. (noise, makes, my neighbor, a lot of)

➡ _____

9 우리는 물고기를 많이 잡지 못했다. (fish, we, catch, many, didn't)

➡ _____

10 Anny는 숙제를 많이 하지 않았다. (didn't, Anny, much, do, homework)

➡ _____

UNIT 01 부사의 쓰임

A ( ) 안에서 알맞은 것을 고르세요.

1 Jerome is very (kind, kindly).

2 Cut the paper (careful, carefully).

3 The car drove (so fast, so fastly) on the road.

4 The baby fell asleep (easy, easily).

5 (Lucky, Luckily), everyone was safe.

6 The stars are shining (beautiful, beautifully) in the sky.

7 She can swim (good, well) in the sea.

8 The man looks (healthy, healthily) and strong.

9 The door shut (sudden, suddenly).

10 The player hit the ball very (hard, hardly).

11 (Strange, Strangely), the windows were open.

12 James looked very (sad, sadly) this morning.

13 Please speak (quiet, quietly) in the library.

14 My grandfather gets up (early, earily) every morning.

15 He (serious, seriously) watched the news.

부사의 쓰임

Answer Key p.24

B 주어진 말을 이용하되 밑줄 친 부분을 바르게 고쳐 우리말을 영어로 바꿔 쓰세요.

1 그는 천천히 차를 마셨다. (drink the tea, slow)

➡ _____

2 그 아이들은 시끄럽게 웃었다. (laugh, loud)

➡ _____

3 그는 그 공을 높이 던졌다. (throw, highly)

➡ _____

4 식물은 사막에서 잘 자라지 않는다. (plants, grow good, in the desert)

➡ _____

5 그녀는 파티를 빨리 떠났다. (left, party, quick)

➡ _____

6 우리는 그것에 대해 다르게 생각한다. (think different about)

➡ _____

7 그녀는 무대에서 아주 아름답게 춤을 췄다. (so beautiful, on the stage)

➡ _____

8 Josh는 그의 형에게 화를 내며 소리쳤다. (shout angry at)

➡ _____

9 우리는 시험을 위해 아주 열심히 공부했다. (very hardly, for the test)

➡ _____

10 Erin은 그녀의 이웃에게 상냥하게 안부 인사를 했다. (say hello to, nice)

➡ _____

A 밑줄 친 부분이 맞으면 O를 쓰고, <u>틀리면</u> 바르게 고치세요.

1 I <u>go often fishing</u> with my dad. → _____

2 Sarah <u>eats never</u> vegetables. → _____

3 He <u>is usually</u> busy with his work. → _____

4 We <u>have sometimes</u> pizza for lunch. → _____

5 We <u>don't rarely play</u> soccer. → _____

6 Harry <u>always is</u> nice to everyone. → _____

7 Does it <u>never snow</u> in Saudi Arabia? → _____

8 The sun <u>always rises</u> in the east. → _____

9 The refrigerator <u>rarely is</u> empty. → _____

10 Is <u>he late often</u> for class? → _____

11 I <u>sometimes am</u> tired after school. → _____

12 I <u>will never forget</u> his face. → _____

13 She <u>often is curious</u> about new things. → _____

14 Does she <u>have usually</u> breakfast? → _____

15 We <u>will always remember</u> that day. → _____

B 주어진 말을 이용하여 우리말을 영어로 바꿔 쓰세요.

1 그들은 거의 등산을 하지 않는다. (climb the mountain)

→ _____

2 그녀는 항상 그녀의 친구들에게 친절하다. (kind, to, friends)

→ _____

3 나는 대개 저녁 식사 후에 개를 산책시킨다. (walk one's dog)

→ _____

4 나의 가족은 가끔 토요일에 캠핑을 간다. (go camping)

→ _____

5 그 쇼핑몰은 자주 사람들로 붐빈다. (mall, crowded with)

→ _____

6 당신은 보통 늦게 잠을 자나요? (go to bed)

→ _____

7 나는 그 식당을 결코 다시 방문하지 않을 것이다. (restaurant, again)

→ _____

8 너는 점심 식사 후에 가끔 졸리니? (sleepy)

→ _____

9 우리는 도시에서는 거의 별을 보지 못한다. (see stars, city)

→ _____

10 그는 항상 지하철을 타고 직장에 간다. (take, subway, to work)

→ _____

When, Where, Why

A   (   ) 안에서 알맞은 것을 고르세요.

1   (When, Where) does the concert start? – At 7:00 P.M.

2   (When, Why) do you look sad? – Because my puppy is sick.

3   (When, Where) are you going on vacation? – I'm going to the beach.

4   (When, Why) did you arrive here? – Yesterday.

5   (Where, Why) did you buy the toy? – Because tomorrow is my son's birthday.

6   (When, Where) is the bookstore? – It's next to the library.

7   (When, Why) is Kate's birthday party? – It's this Friday.

8   (Where, When) do you usually drink coffee? – At the café over there.

9   (When, Why) are you closing the window? – It's raining outside.

10   (When, Where) does the museum close? – At 6:00 P.M.

11   (Why, Where) does your dog like to sleep? – On the sofa.

12   (Why, Where) did he go to Singapore? – For work.

13   (Where, When) do you wake up in the morning? – At 7:30.

14   (Where, Why) is the Louvre Museum? – It's in Paris.

15   (When, Why) do you like him? – He is kind and handsome.

Answer Key p.25

B 주어진 말을 이용하여 우리말을 영어로 바꿔 쓰세요.

1 너는 네 가방을 어디에서 잃어버렸니? (lose your bag)

➡ _____

2 너는 오늘 왜 기분이 좋니? (feeling happy)

➡ _____

3 당신은 언제 캐나다에 방문했나요? (visit Canada)

➡ _____

4 왜 그는 당신에게 화가 났었나요? (be angry at)

➡ _____

5 네 형은 어디에서 일하니? (your brother)

➡ _____

6 너는 언제 그 선물을 받았니? (get the present)

➡ _____

7 너는 어디에서 태어났니? (be born)

➡ _____

8 너는 언제 조깅하러 가니? (go jogging)

➡ _____

9 Charles는 왜 그렇게 피곤해 보이니? (so tired)

➡ _____

10 여름 방학은 언제 시작하니? (summer vacation, start)

➡ _____

A 빈칸에 who, what 중에서 알맞은 의문사를 골라 쓰세요.

1 _____ is the man over there? – He is my uncle.

2 _____ are you doing this Saturday? – I'm going to go fishing.

3 _____ music do you like? – I like dance music.

4 _____ are you waiting for? – I'm waiting for Karen.

5 _____ did she cook for dinner? – She cooked chicken soup.

6 _____ helped you with your project? – Julie helped me.

7 _____ time does the show start? – It starts at 5:30.

8 _____ cleaned the house? – My dad and I did.

9 _____ is your favorite color? – I like blue.

10 _____ did you meet yesterday? – I met my cousin Sarah.

11 _____ size do you want? – A size 6, please.

12 _____ sport do you like? – I like volleyball.

13 _____ do you think about the movie? – It is boring.

14 _____ went shopping with you? – My mom.

15 _____ did you invite to your birthday party? – I invited Ken, Sam, and Kate.

Answer Key p.25

B 주어진 말을 이용하여 우리말을 영어로 바꿔 쓰세요.

1 소파 위에 무엇이 있나요? (the sofa)

➡ _____

2 누가 그 퀴즈를 풀었나요? (solve the quiz)

➡ _____

3 당신은 어젯밤에 누구에게 전화했나요? (call last night)

➡ _____

4 그 아이들이 거기에서 무엇을 만들고 있나요? (make there)

➡ _____

5 누가 당신에게 그 멋진 선물을 보냈나요? (send you, nice gift)

➡ _____

6 당신은 아침 식사로 주로 무엇을 먹나요? (eat for breakfast)

➡ _____

7 너의 꿈의 직업은 뭐니? (dream job)

➡ _____

8 누가 노래를 크게 부르고 있니? (the song, loudly)

➡ _____

9 너는 누구와 함께 노는 것을 좋아하니? (play with)

➡ _____

10 너는 동물원에서 무엇을 봤니? (see, at the zoo)

➡ _____

A 대화가 완성되도록 빈칸에 알맞은 말을 쓰세요.

1 _____ _____ your weekend? – It was great.

2 _____ _____ you go to the airport? – By subway.

3 _____ _____ did they dance? – They danced great.

4 _____ _____ do you eat hamburgers? – I eat them once a week.

5 _____ _____ is it from here to the beach? – It's 1 kilometer from here.

6 _____ _____ is the river? – It's about 50 kilometers long.

7 _____ _____ you know it? – My friend told me.

8 _____ _____ is the building? – It's about 30 meters tall.

9 _____ _____ is your grandfather? – He is 72 years old.

10 _____ _____ is the watermelon? – It's almost the size of a soccer ball.

11 _____ _____ are you going to stay here? – For three days.

12 _____ _____ the food? – It was delicious.

13 _____ _____ does it rain in summer? – About once a week.

14 _____ _____ is the big tree? – It's about 100 years old.

15 _____ _____ you like your steak? – I like my steak well done.

Answer Key p.25

B 주어진 말을 바르게 배열하여 문장을 완성하세요.

1 그 쇼핑몰은 얼마나 큰가요? (is, how, the shopping mall, big)

➡ _____

2 여기서 우체국은 얼마나 먼가요? (here, how, the post office, far, is, from)

➡ _____

3 당신은 오늘 기분이 어떤가요? (you, how, today, feeling, are)

➡ _____

4 너의 가족은 얼마나 자주 외식을 하니? (your family, how, does, eat out, often)

➡ _____

5 저기에 다리는 얼마나 오래됐나요? (how, over there, is, old, the bridge)

➡ _____

6 그는 시험에서 얼마나 잘했나요? (how, on the test, did, he, well, do)

➡ _____

7 네 남동생은 키가 얼마나 크니? (is, how, little brother, tall, your)

➡ _____

8 너는 어떻게 이런 멋진 식당을 찾았어? (find, how, did, this nice restaurant, you)

➡ _____

9 거기에 도착하는 데 얼마나 오래 걸렸나요? (take, how, it, long, to get there, did)

➡ _____

10 어떻게 그들은 숙제를 빨리 끝냈지? (finish, did, they, how, the homework quickly)

➡ _____

UNIT 01 셀 수 있는 명사

단어	뜻	단어 쓰기	뜻 쓰기
01 elephant	몡 코끼리		
02 island	몡 섬		
03 watermelon	몡 수박		
04 potato	몡 감자		
05 wolf	몡 늑대		
06 knife	몡 칼		
07 tooth	몡 이, 치아		
08 sheep	몡 양		
09 deer	몡 사슴		
10 fox	몡 여우		
11 country	몡 나라		
12 leaf	몡 (나뭇)잎		
13 spider	몡 거미		
14 match	몡 성냥		
15 neighbor	몡 이웃 (사람)		
16 chat	통 이야기를 나누다, 수다를 떨다		
17 strawberry	몡 딸기		
18 eraser	몡 지우개		

19	rose	명 장미		
20	dangerous	형 위험한		
21	sharp	형 날카로운		
22	kitten	명 새끼 고양이		
23	princess	명 공주		
24	son	명 아들		
25	daughter	명 딸		
26	peach	명 복숭아		
27	pick	동 따다, 뜯다		
28	forest	명 숲		
29	farm	명 농장		
30	carrot	명 당근		

UNIT 02 셀 수 없는 명사

단어		뜻	단어 쓰기	뜻 쓰기
01	peace	명 평화		
02	luck	명 운, 행운		
03	beauty	명 아름다움		
04	oil	명 기름		
05	meat	명 고기		
06	soap	명 비누		
07	salt	명 소금		

08	sugar	명 설탕		
09	pepper	명 후추		
10	rice	명 쌀, 밥		
11	mail	명 우편(물)		
12	sweet	형 달콤한		
13	baker	명 제빵사		
14	pocket	명 주머니		
15	piece	명 조각, 쪽		
16	bottle	명 병		
17	bowl	명 그릇, 사발		
18	slice	명 (얇게 썬) 조각		
19	loaf	명 덩어리 a loaf of bread 빵 한 덩어리		
20	order	동 주문하다		
21	gift	명 선물		
22	interesting	형 흥미로운		
23	animal	명 동물		
24	put	동 놓다, 두다		
25	bake	동 굽다		
26	dessert	명 디저트, 후식		
27	important	형 중요한		
28	paper	명 종이		
29	helpful	형 도움이 되는		
30	mix	동 섞다, 섞이다		

Chapter 02

다음 단어들을 잘 듣고 따라 쓴 후 그 뜻을 쓰세요.

UNIT 01 인칭대명사

단어	뜻	단어 쓰기	뜻 쓰기
01 teach	동 가르치다		
02 sport	명 운동, 스포츠		
03 smart	형 똑똑한		
04 purse	명 (여성용) 지갑		
05 watch	명 손목시계 동 보다		
06 flower	명 꽃		
07 problem	명 문제		
08 best	형 최고의		
09 street	명 거리, 도로		
10 badminton	명 배드민턴		
11 wash	동 씻다		
12 everyone	명 모든 사람, 모두		
13 fur	명 (동물의) 털, 모피		
14 black	명 검정색 형 검은		
15 husband	명 남편		
16 spend	동 (돈을) 쓰다; (시간을) 보내다		
17 vacation	명 방학, 휴가		
18 hurt	동 다치게 하다		

		단어 쓰기	뜻 쓰기
19 wife	명 아내		
20 ask	동 묻다		
21 yellow	명 노란색 형 노란색의		
22 hate	동 싫어하다		
23 scary	형 무서운		
24 meal	명 식사 after a meal 식후에		
25 generous	형 너그러운		
26 money	명 돈		
27 bark	동 짖다 bark at ~를 보고 짖다		
28 last name	명 성, 성씨		
29 brown	명 갈색 형 갈색의		
30 dictionary	명 사전		

UNIT 02 지시대명사

단어	뜻	단어 쓰기	뜻 쓰기
01 expensive	형 비싼		
02 notebook	명 공책		
03 gloves	명 장갑		
04 mittens	명 벙어리 장갑		
05 doll	명 인형		
06 necklace	명 목걸이		
07 sneakers	명 운동화		

08	gold	명 금		
09	towel	명 수건		
10	suit	명 정장		
11	rainbow	명 무지개		
12	magazine	명 잡지		
13	vegetable	명 채소		
14	word	명 단어; 말		
15	boots	명 부츠		
16	homeroom teacher	명 담임 선생님		
17	wet	형 젖은		
18	perfume	명 향수		
19	blanket	명 담요		
20	warm	형 따뜻한		
21	shoes	명 신발		
22	actor	명 배우		
23	sweater	명 스웨터		
24	empty	형 비어 있는, 빈		
25	soup	명 수프		
26	earrings	명 귀걸이		
27	smell	동 ~ 냄새[향]가 나다		
28	pencil case	명 필통		
29	sour	형 (맛이) 신		
30	butterfly	명 나비		

UNIT 01 There is / are

단어	뜻	단어 쓰기	뜻 쓰기
01 **garden**	명 정원		
02 **button**	명 단추		
03 **plate**	명 접시		
04 **ruler**	명 자		
05 **shelf**	명 선반		
06 **coin**	명 동전		
07 **bedroom**	명 침실		
08 **movie theater**	명 극장		
09 **near**	전 ~ 근처에		
10 **elevator**	명 엘리베이터		
11 **clock**	명 시계		
12 **wall**	명 벽 on the wall 벽에		
13 **lighthouse**	명 등대		
14 **bathroom**	명 욕실, 화장실		
15 **parrot**	명 앵무새		
16 **cage**	명 새장, 우리		
17 **zebra**	명 얼룩말		
18 **grass**	명 풀, 잔디(밭)		

단어	뜻	단어 쓰기	뜻 쓰기
19 wallet	몡 지갑		
20 aquarium	몡 수족관		
21 corner	몡 모서리, 모퉁이 on the corner 길모퉁이에		
22 calendar	몡 달력		
23 jewelry	몡 보석(류)		
24 hole	몡 구멍		
25 playground	몡 놀이터		
26 teapot	몡 찻주전자		
27 mistake	몡 실수		
28 outside	분 밖에, 밖에서		
29 jar	몡 병, 단지		
30 airport	몡 공항		

UNIT 02 비인칭 주어 It

단어	뜻	단어 쓰기	뜻 쓰기
01 lamp	몡 전등, 스탠드		
02 sunny	혱 화창한, 햇살이 내리쬐는		
03 clear	혱 (날씨가) 맑은		
04 spring	몡 봄		
05 summer	몡 여름		
06 fall	몡 가을 (= autumn)		
07 winter	몡 겨울		

08	kilometer	명 킬로미터		
09	rain	명 비 동 비가 오다		
10	snow	명 눈 동 눈이 오다		
11	river	명 강		
12	far	형 (거리가) 먼		
13	from A to B	A부터 B까지		
14	humid	형 습한		
15	national	형 국가의 national holiday 국경일		
16	windy	형 바람이 많이 부는		
17	present	명 선물		
18	under	전 ~ 아래에		
19	still	부 여전히		
20	inside	전 ~ 안에		
21	pond	명 연못		
22	middle	명 중앙, (한)가운데 in the middle of ~의 중앙에		
23	air	명 공기		
24	let's	~하자 Let's go. 가자.		
25	strong	형 강한, 튼튼한 strong wind 강풍		
26	foggy	형 안개가 낀		
27	first	형 첫째의 명 첫, 첫째		
28	anniversary	명 기념일 wedding anniversary 결혼 기념일		
29	only	부 오직, 겨우		
30	already	부 벌써, 이미		

Chapter 04

다음 단어들을 잘 듣고 따라 쓴 후 그 뜻을 쓰세요.

UNIT 01 형용사의 쓰임

단어	뜻	단어 쓰기	뜻 쓰기
01 purple	형 자주색의		
02 seawater	명 바닷물		
03 salty	형 (맛이) 짠		
04 writer	명 작가		
05 castle	명 성		
06 chicken	명 닭, 닭고기		
07 thick	형 두꺼운		
08 medicine	명 약		
09 bitter	형 (맛이) 쓴		
10 colorful	형 형형색색의, 다채로운		
11 balloon	명 풍선		
12 ugly	형 못생긴, 추한		
13 pumpkin	명 호박		
14 soft	형 부드러운, 푹신한		
15 lovely	형 사랑스러운, 예쁜		
16 turtle	명 거북이		
17 clever	형 영리한		
18 round	형 둥근		

19	healthy	형 건강한, 건강에 좋은		
20	nurse	명 간호사		
21	safe	형 안전한		
22	neck	명 목		
23	ladder	명 사다리		
24	pillow	명 베개		
25	person	명 사람		
26	popular	형 인기 있는		
27	businessman	명 사업가		
28	bored	형 지루해하는		
29	different	형 다른		
30	smooth	형 부드러운, 매끈한		

UNIT 02 수량형용사

단어		뜻	단어 쓰기	뜻 쓰기
01	many	형 (수가) 많은		
02	much	형 (양이) 많은		
03	a lot of	형 (수·양이) 많은		
04	picture	명 그림; 사진		
05	some	형 약간의		
06	any	형 어떤, 조금도		
07	need	동 필요하다		

08	want	통 원하다		
09	poem	명 시		
10	time	명 시간		
11	noise	명 소음 make noise 시끄럽게 하다		
12	teacher	명 선생님		
13	song	명 노래		
14	soda	명 탄산음료		
15	free time	명 여가[자유] 시간		
16	building	명 건물		
17	message	명 메시지		
18	fail	통 (시험에) 떨어지다, 낙제하다		
19	plan	명 계획		
20	weekend	명 주말		
21	cherry	명 체리		
22	in front of	전 ~ 앞에		
23	save	통 모으다, 저축하다		
24	clothes	명 옷, 의복		
25	pass	통 합격하다; 건네주다		
26	strange	형 이상한		
27	suitcase	명 여행 가방		
28	subject	명 과목		
29	wise	형 현명한		
30	sunshine	명 햇빛		

Chapter 05

다음 단어들을 잘 듣고 따라 쓴 후 그 뜻을 쓰세요.

UNIT 01 부사의 쓰임

단어	뜻	단어 쓰기	뜻 쓰기
01 quietly	📢 조용히		
02 lose	📢 지다; 잃어버리다		
03 luckily	📢 운 좋게		
04 snail	📢 달팽이		
05 slowly	📢 느리게		
06 carefully	📢 조심스럽게		
07 quickly	📢 빨리, 빠르게		
08 fast	📢 빠른 📢 빨리, 빠르게		
09 high	📢 높은 📢 높이, 높게		
10 well	📢 잘		
11 great	📢 위대한, 훌륭한		
12 serious	📢 심각한, 진지한		
13 ankle	📢 발목		
14 wake up	(잠에서) 깨다		
15 suddenly	📢 갑자기		
16 solve	📢 풀다, 해결하다		
17 dream	📢 꿈 📢 꿈을 꾸다		
18 look	📢 ~해 보이다		

단어	뜻	단어 쓰기	뜻 쓰기
19 **frog**	명 개구리		
20 **jump**	동 뛰어오르다		
21 **pollution**	명 오염 air pollution 대기 오염		
22 **snore**	동 코를 골다		
23 **greet**	동 인사하다		
24 **polite**	형 예의 바른, 공손한		
25 **anything**	명 무엇, 아무것		
26 **surprisingly**	부 놀랍게도		
27 **shout**	동 소리치다		
28 **guitar**	명 기타 play the guitar 기타를 치다		
29 **return**	동 반납하다		
30 **raise**	동 올리다 raise one's hand 손을 들다		

UNIT 02 빈도부사

단어	뜻	단어 쓰기	뜻 쓰기
01 **sometimes**	부 가끔, 때때로		
02 **rarely**	부 거의 ~않다		
03 **never**	부 결코 ~않다		
04 **same**	형 똑같은		
05 **eat out**	외식하다		
06 **pool**	명 수영장 (= swimming pool)		
07 **nervous**	형 불안한, 초조한		

08	interview	몡 면접		
09	kindness	몡 친절		
10	on time	정시에		
11	cheerful	혱 쾌활한		
12	surf	동 인터넷을 검색하다 surf the Internet 인터넷을 검색하다		
13	midnight	몡 자정 at midnight 자정에		
14	crowded	혱 붐비는		
15	afternoon	몡 오후		
16	nap	몡 낮잠 take a nap 낮잠을 자다		
17	laundry	몡 세탁, 빨래 do the laundry 빨래를 하다		
18	Saturday	몡 토요일		
19	radio	몡 라디오		
20	again	붬 다시		
21	skip	동 거르다		
22	friendly	혱 친절한, 상냥한		
23	wear	동 입다; 쓰다		
24	sunglasses	몡 선글라스		
25	give up	포기하다		
26	prize	몡 상		
27	enter	동 들어가다		
28	lift	동 들어올리다		
29	find	동 찾다, 발견하다		
30	act	동 연기하다		

Chapter 06

다음 단어들을 잘 듣고 따라 쓴 후 그 뜻을 쓰세요.

UNIT 01 When, Where, Why

단어	뜻	단어 쓰기	뜻 쓰기
01 when	언제		
02 where	어디에(서)		
03 why	왜		
04 because	웹 ~ 때문에		
05 miss	동 놓치다		
06 cry	동 울다		
07 test	명 시험, 검사		
08 lunchtime	명 점심시간		
09 festival	명 축제		
10 field trip	명 견학 여행, 현장 학습		
11 cafeteria	명 구내식당, 카페테리아		
12 absent	형 결석한		
13 skirt	명 치마		
14 come from	~ 출신이다 (= be from)		
15 dentist	명 치과의사, 치과		
16 toothache	명 치통 have a toothache 이가 아프다		
17 folk village	명 민속촌		
18 driver	명 운전자		

19	stop	통 멈추다		
20	red light	빨간 신호등 (= red traffic light)		
21	wedding	명 결혼(식)		
22	excited	형 신이 난, 들뜬		
23	call	통 전화하다; 부르다		
24	grow up	성장하다, 자라다		
25	send	통 보내다		
26	City Hall	명 시청		
27	drugstore	명 약국		
28	concert	명 연주회, 콘서트		
29	quit	통 그만두다		
30	job	명 직장, 일자리		

UNIT 02 Who, What

단어		뜻	단어 쓰기	뜻 쓰기
01	who	누구		
02	what	무엇		
03	kitchen	명 부엌, 주방		
04	T-shirt	명 티셔츠		
05	color	명 색		
06	pot	명 화분		
07	furniture	명 가구		

08	happen	동 발생하다, 일어나다		
09	accident	명 사고		
10	win	동 이기다		
11	race	명 경주, 레이스		
12	frame	명 액자		
13	fall off	~에서 떨어지다		
14	invent	동 발명하다		
15	briefcase	명 서류 가방		
16	lottery	명 복권 win the lottery 복권에 당첨되다		
17	talk to	~와 이야기하다		
18	design	동 디자인[설계]하다		
19	hide and seek	명 숨바꼭질 play hide and seek 숨바꼭질하다		
20	aunt	명 이모, 고모, 숙모		
21	light	명 전등		
22	ceiling	명 천장		
23	drop	동 떨어뜨리다		
24	handkerchief	명 손수건		
25	grade	동 채점하다		
26	do the dishes	설거지하다		
27	drawer	명 서랍		
28	clean	동 닦다, 청소하다		
29	address	명 주소		
30	phone number	명 전화번호		

UNIT 03 How

단어	뜻	단어 쓰기	뜻 쓰기
01 **how**	어떻게, 어떤		
02 **fantastic**	형 굉장한, 멋진		
03 **fix**	동 고치다, 수리하다		
04 **repairman**	명 수리공		
05 **date**	명 데이트 동 데이트하다		
06 **terrible**	형 끔찍한		
07 **exercise**	동 운동하다		
08 **tower**	명 탑		
09 **speak**	동 이야기하다, 말하다		
10 **gracefully**	부 우아하게		
11 **centimeter**	명 센티미터		
12 **temple**	명 절, 사원		
13 **hundred**	명 백, 100		
14 **hour**	명 시간		
15 **grocery**	명 식료품 do grocery shopping 장을 보다		
16 **once a week**	일주일에 한 번		
17 **travel**	동 여행하다		
18 **hospital**	명 병원		
19 **P.E. class**	명 체육 수업		
20 **station**	명 역		

21	**stay**	동 머무르다, 지내다		
22	**weather**	명 날씨		
23	**palace**	명 궁전		
24	**gas station**	명 주유소		
25	**show**	명 쇼, 공연		
26	**subway**	명 지하철		
27	**recipe**	명 조리법		
28	**get a haircut**	머리를 자르다		
29	**puzzle**	명 퍼즐, 수수께끼		
30	**in a hurry**	서둘러; 바쁜		

Grammar +Plus Writing

START

Grammar +Plus Writing

START

ANSWER KEY 2

Chapter 01 명사

UNIT 01 셀 수 있는 명사

PRACTICE 1   p.10

1 a	**2** a	**3** an
4 a	**5** an	**6** a
7 a	**8** an	

해설

자음으로 시작하는 단수 명사 앞에는 a, 모음(a, e, i, o, u)으로 시작하는 단수 명사 앞에는 an을 붙인다. h, w는 자음이므로 an을 쓰지 않도록 주의한다.

PRACTICE 2   p.11

1 pencils	**2** foxes	**3** countries
4 leaves	**5** women	**6** mice
7 teeth	**8** sheep	

해설

대부분의 셀 수 있는 명사는 -s를 붙여 복수형을 만들고, -sh, -ch, -s, -x, -o로 끝나는 명사는 -es를 붙인다. 「자음+y」로 끝나는 명사는 y를 i로 고치고 -es를 붙이며, -f, -fe로 끝나는 명사는 -f, -fe를 v로 고치고 -es를 붙인다. 이외에 불규칙한 복수형은 따로 외워두도록 한다.

문법 쏙쏙   pp.12~13

A

1 house	**2** boy	**3** days
4 friends	**5** egg	**6** glasses
7 legs	**8** matches	**9** neighbor
10 jeans	**11** sister, brothers	
12 teeth	**13** women	**14** strawberries
15 an eraser		

해설

1, 2, 5, 9, 11 > '하나'를 뜻하는 a/an 뒤에는 단수 명사가 온다.
3, 4, 7, 8, 11, 13, 14 > 둘 이상의 개수를 나타내는 말 뒤에는 복수 명사가 온다.
6, 10 > 쌍을 이루는 명사 glasses(안경), jeans(청바지), shoes(신발), pants(바지), socks(양말), gloves(장갑) 등은 항상 복수형으로 쓴다.
12 > '양치하다'라고 말할 때는 tooth의 복수형 teeth를 쓴다.
15 > 모음으로 시작하는 단수 명사 앞에는 an을 쓴다.

B

1 potatoes	**2** roses	**3** tickets
4 sheep	**5** keys	**6** Wolves
7 mice	**8** beaches	**9** knives
10 fish	**11** countries	**12** Deer
13 kittens	**14** buses	**15** dresses

해설

1, 8, 14, 15 > -sh, -ch, -s, -x, -o로 끝나는 명사는 -es를 붙인다.
2, 3, 5, 13 > 대부분의 명사는 -s를 붙여 복수형을 만든다.
4, 10, 12 > sheep, fish, deer는 단수형과 복수형이 같다.
6, 9 > wolf, knife는 -f, -fe로 끝나므로 -f, -fe를 v로 고치고 -es를 붙인다.
7 > mouse는 불규칙 명사로 복수형은 mice이다.
11 > country는 「자음+y」로 끝나므로 y를 i로 고치고 -es를 붙인다.

영작 술술   pp.14~15

A

1 The couple has a son and two daughters.
2 She is wearing three rings.
3 Do you like peaches?
4 The woman is walking with her two dogs.
5 Jack has a house near the beach.
6 Leaves fall in autumn.
7 Ann picked an orange from a tree.
8 We saw three deer in the forest.
9 Two men are fighting on the street.
10 Does the shop sell scarves?

B

1 The book has 200 pages.
2 I had a hamburger for lunch.
3 My grandfather grows sweet potatoes.
4 We saw many sheep on the farm.
5 The baby has two teeth.
6 I have an English book.
7 I bought an onion and two carrots.
8 Ian and Amy have two children.
9 She visited many cities in Europe.
10 He put the boxes on the table.

A

1 Big cities are usually noisy.
2 I bought some tomatoes.
3 He is carrying two boxes.
4 Jejudo is an island.
5 All the dishes are dirty.
6 Many wolves live in America.
7 The children are playing with a ball.

해설

1 ▸ city는 「자음+y」로 끝나므로 y를 i로 고치고 -es를 붙인다.
2, 3, 5 ▸ tomato, box, dish는 -o, -x, -sh로 끝나므로 -es를 붙인다.
4 ▸ island는 모음(i)으로 시작하므로 an을 붙인다.
6 ▸ wolf는 f로 끝나므로 f를 v로 고치고 -es를 붙인다.
7 ▸ child의 복수형은 children이다.

B

1 Three foxes are in the cage.
2 Men and women are very different.
3 Her teeth are very white.
4 We visited five countries last year.
5 He has an aunt in Busan.

C 1 ③ 2 ①

해설

1 ▸ hat은 자음(h)으로 시작하므로 a를 붙인다.
2 ▸ fish는 단수형(a fish)과 복수형(many fish)이 같다.

개념 Review

❶ 셀 수 있는 명사 ❷ 셀 수 없는 명사 ❸ a
❹ an ❺ -s/-es ❻ 불규칙한

UNIT 02 셀 수 없는 명사

PRACTICE 1 p.18

1 Sugar 2 bread
3 coffee 4 money

해설

셀 수 없는 명사는 a/an을 붙이거나 복수형을 만들 수 없다.

PRACTICE 2 p.19

1 loaf 2 cups
3 box 4 bowl

해설

셀 수 없는 명사는 모양(piece, slice, loaf, bar…)이나 담는 그릇(cup, glass, bottle, bowl, box…)을 단위로 해서 수량을 표현할 수 있다. 이때 단위 명사는 a/an을 붙이거나 복수형을 만들 수 있다.

문법 쏙쏙 pp.20~21

A

1 셀 수 없는 명사	2 셀 수 없는 명사
3 셀 수 있는 명사	4 셀 수 없는 명사
5 셀 수 없는 명사	6 셀 수 있는 명사
7 셀 수 없는 명사	8 셀 수 없는 명사
9 셀 수 있는 명사	10 셀 수 없는 명사
11 셀 수 없는 명사	12 셀 수 없는 명사
13 셀 수 있는 명사	14 셀 수 없는 명사
15 셀 수 있는 명사	

해설

1 ▸ coin(동전), bill(지폐) 등은 셀 수 있지만, money는 돈을 통칭하는 말로 셀 수 없는 명사에 속한다.
2, 4, 12 ▸ music, work, luck은 추상적인 개념으로 셀 수 없는 명사에 속한다.
3, 6, 9, 13, 15 ▸ song, son, letter, chair, animal은 모두 셀 수 있는 명사로 단수일 때 a/an을 붙이거나 복수일 때 복수형을 만든다.
5, 8, 11 ▸ chocolate, water, orange juice 등 모양이 일정하지 않은 고체나 액체류는 셀 수 없는 명사에 속한다.
7 ▸ London과 같은 지명은 고유 명사로 셀 수 없는 명사이다.
10 ▸ letter(편지)는 셀 수 있지만, mail은 우편물 전체를 의미하므로 셀 수 없는 명사에 속한다.
14 ▸ salt와 같이 너무 작아 셀 수 없는 것은 셀 수 없는 명사에 속한다.

B

1 a cup of	2 a loaf of
3 a piece of	4 A bottle of
5 a slice of	6 a glass of
7 three bowls of	8 a bar of
9 a cup of	10 a glass of
11 four loaves of	12 a box of
13 two bars of	14 A bowl of
15 a piece of	

1, 9 ‘차 한 잔,’ ‘커피 한 잔’은 cup을 단위로 사용한다.

2, 11 ‘빵 한 덩어리’는 loaf를 단위로 사용하며, 복수형은 loaves이다.

3, 15 ‘치즈 한 조각’, ‘케이크 한 조각’은 piece를 단위로 사용한다.

4, 6, 10 lemonade, juice, milk 등은 bottle이나 glass를 단위로 사용한다.

5 ‘치즈 한 장’은 a slice of cheese이다.

7, 14 ‘수프 한 그릇,’ ‘밥 한 공기’는 bowl을 단위로 사용한다.

8, 13 ‘초콜릿 한 개’, ‘비누 한 개’는 bar를 단위로 사용한다.

12 ‘사탕 한 상자’는 a box of candy이다.

영작 술술

pp.22~23

A

1 We don't have much <u>time</u>.

2 <u>Love</u> is important to everyone.

3 Justin likes rock <u>music</u>.

4 Brian has too much <u>work</u> to do.

5 Thank you for your <u>advice</u>.

6 I put some <u>butter</u> on my bread.

7 Jim had <u>a bowl of</u> rice with kimchi.

8 You need <u>two slices of</u> bread for a sandwich.

9 I would like <u>a cup of</u> coffee, please.

10 He ordered a hamburger and <u>a glass of</u> juice.

B

1 We have too much homework.

2 Emily listens to music every day.

3 Do mice like cheese?

4 Money is not everything.

5 July 1 is Sunday.

6 She eats a lot of fruit.

7 I need some furniture in my room.

8 I drink eight glasses of water a day.

9 Cathy bought two bars of soap.

10 Mark enjoys two cups of tea a day.

WRAP UP

pp.24~25

A

1 Everybody wants peace.

2 I drank a glass[bottle / cup] of water.

3 Seoul is a big city.

4 I ordered a bowl of cream soup.

5 He doesn't have any money.

6 I had two cups of coffee today.

7 We ate four bars of chocolate.

1 peace(평화)는 셀 수 없는 명사로 복수형을 만들 수 없다.

2 water는 glass나 bottle, cup을 단위로 사용한다.

3 Seoul은 고유 명사로 a를 붙일 수 없다.

4 soup는 bowl을 단위로 사용한다.

5 money는 셀 수 없는 명사로 복수형을 만들 수 없다.

6 ‘커피 두 잔’이므로 cup은 복수형인 cups가 되어야 한다.

7 chocolate은 셀 수 없는 명사로 a를 붙이거나 복수형을 만들 수 없다. 복수형은 단위 명사를 복수로 쓴다.

B

1 I need a piece of paper.

2 Your advice was helpful.

3 She has some mail from America.

4 I am going to buy a loaf of bread.

5 Water and oil don't mix.

C   **1** ②   **2** ③

1 ① An apple juice → Apple juice ③ a sugar → sugar ④ musics → music이 알맞다.

2 bread는 셀 수 없는 명사로 a를 붙이거나 복수형을 만들 수 없으며, ‘빵 두 조각’은 two pieces of bread로 나타낸다.

개념 Review

❶ 단수   ❷ 모양   ❸ 담는 그릇

❹ 단위 명사

ACTUAL TEST

pp.26~27

01 ④	02 ④	03 ②	04 ③
05 ③	06 ③	07 ②	08 ③

09 ①

10 People have two feet.

11 My teacher gave me a lot of advice.

12 ③   13 ①

14 They need food and water.

15 George is brushing his teeth.

01 baby는 「자음+y」로 끝나므로 y를 i로 고치고 -es를 붙인다.

02 ‘치즈 두 장’은 two slices of cheese로 표현한다.

03 window는 자음 ‘w’로 시작하므로 앞에 a를 붙인다.

04 city는 셀 수 있는 명사이고, 도시 하나를 의미하므로 a city 가 알맞다.

05 a 뒤에는 셀 수 있는 단수 명사가 온다. ① soup은 셀 수 없는 명사이고, ② apple은 an apple이어야 하며, ④ sand-wiches는 복수이므로 쓸 수 없다.

06 tomato의 복수형은 tomatoes이다.

07 rice는 셀 수 없는 명사로 a를 붙일 수 없으므로 a rice는 rice로 고쳐야 한다.

08 kangaroo와 animal은 셀 수 있는 명사로 a kangaroo, an animal이 알맞고, 국가 이름은 고유 명사로 a/an을 붙이지 않는다.

09 bread와 butter는 셀 수 없는 명사로 복수형을 만들 수 없다.

10 foot의 복수형은 feet이다.

11 advice는 셀 수 없는 명사로 복수형을 만들 수 없다.

12 child의 복수형은 children이다. ④ sheep은 단수형과 복수형이 같다.

13 '수프 한 그릇'은 a bowl of soup이다. a loaf of는 '한 덩어리의'라는 뜻으로 bread와 쓸 수 있다.

14 '음식(food)'과 '물(water)'은 모두 셀 수 없는 명사로 a/an을 붙일 수 없고 복수형을 쓰지 않는다.

15 '이를 닦다'는 tooth의 복수형을 사용해 brush one's teeth로 표현한다.

Chapter 02 대명사

UNIT 01 인칭대명사

PRACTICE 1   p.30

1 It	**2** They
3 her	**4** me

해설

인칭대명사의 주격은 I/we/you/he/she/it/they로 주어(~은/는)를 대신한다. 목적격은 me/us/you/him/her/it/them으로 목적어(~을/를)를 대신한다.

PRACTICE 2   p.31

1 my	**2** Your
3 hers	**4** yours

해설

인칭대명사의 소유격(~의)은 my/our/your/his/her/their/its로 항상 뒤에 오는 명사와 함께 쓰인다. 소유대명사(~의 것)는 mine/ours/yours/his/hers/theirs로 「소유격+명사」를 대신

한다. (소유대명사 its는 잘 쓰이지 않음)

문법 쏙쏙   pp.32~33

A

1 They	**2** Your	**3** her
4 It	**5** my	**6** me
7 Their	**8** her	**9** yours
10 Its	**11** his	**12** I
13 them	**14** him	**15** us

해설

1, 4, 12 ▶ 주격(~은/는)이 와야 하므로 They, It, I가 알맞다.

2, 5, 7, 8, 10 ▶ 뒤에 명사가 쓰여 소유격(~의)이 와야 하므로 Your, my, Their, her, Its가 알맞다.

3, 6, 13, 14, 15 ▶ 목적격(~을/를)이 와야 하므로 her, me, them, him, us가 알맞다.

9, 11 ▶ 소유대명사(~의 것)가 와야 하므로 yours, his가 알맞다.

B

1 It	**2** him	**3** theirs
4 it	**5** her	**6** our
7 its	**8** She	**9** his
10 me	**11** their	**12** Ours
13 They	**14** my	**15** her

해설

1, 8, 13 ▶ 주어 자리이므로 인칭대명사의 주격(~은/는)이 온다.

2, 4, 10, 15 ▶ 목적어 자리에는 목적격(~을/를)이 온다.

3, 12 ▶ 뒤에 동사가 있으므로 소유대명사(~의 것) 자리이다.

5, 6, 7, 9, 11, 14 ▶ 뒤에 명사가 나오면 소유격(~의)이 온다.

영작 술술   pp.34~35

A

1 The little boy is <u>my</u> brother.

2 Today is <u>your</u> birthday.

3 We don't know <u>them</u> very well.

4 Peter always helps <u>me</u>.

5 <u>Her</u> parents are generous.

6 The umbrella is <u>hers</u>.

7 A leaf fell from <u>its</u> tree.

8 The money is <u>mine</u>.

9 The dog barked at <u>us</u>.

10 Did he find <u>his</u> shoes?

B

1 Sally is not my sister.

2 Her last name is Kim.

3 Are the books yours?

4 Do you know her?

5 The bag is not his.

6 The baby smiled at him.

7 The children ate their food.

8 John calls me every day.

9 Jack loves his grandmother.

10 Diana invited us to the party.

WRAP UP

pp.36~37

A

1 He lives in New York.

2 Their dog is white.

3 The jacket is hers.

4 Do you know them?

5 We saw Jane and her boyfriend.

6 His eyes are blue. Mine are brown.

7 Do you like our new furniture?

해설

1 ▸ 주어를 대신하므로 His → He

2 ▸ '그들의 개'이므로 Theirs → Their

3 ▸ '그녀의 것'이므로 her → hers

4 ▸ 목적어를 대신하므로 they → them

5 ▸ '그녀의 남자친구'이므로 she → her

6 ▸ '나의 것은 갈색이다.'이므로 '나의 것'은 My → Mine

7 ▸ '우리의 새 가구'이므로 us → our

B

1 They are my cousins.

2 The dictionary is ours.

3 Ted is going to wash his car.

4 My parents love me so much.

5 Mary and I don't like its smell.

C　**1** ①　　　　**2** ②

해설

1 ▸ ② Hers → Her, ③ its → it's[it is], ④ he → him이 알맞다.

2 ▸ 명사 neighbors 앞에는 소유격인 Our(우리의)가 오고, 동사 are 앞에는 Mr. and Mrs. Smith를 대신하는 주어 They(그들은)가 와야 한다.

개념 Review

❶ 인칭대명사　　❷ 주어　　❸ 목적어

❹ 명사　　❺ 소유격 + 명사

UNIT 02 지시대명사

PRACTICE 1

p.38

1 this	**2** That
3 This	**4** that

해설

가리키는 대상이 단수일 때 '이, 이것, 이 사람[분]'은 this, '저, 저 것, 저 사람[분]'은 that을 사용한다.

PRACTICE 2

p.39

1 Those	**2** these
3 These	**4** those

해설

가리키는 대상이 복수일 때 '이, 이것들, 이 사람[분]들'은 these, '저, 저것들, 저 사람[분]들'은 those를 쓴다.

문법 쏙쏙

pp.40~41

A

1 This	**2** That	**3** these
4 That	**5** Those	**6** this
7 these	**8** Those	**9** That
10 These	**11** that	**12** This
13 These	**14** those	**15** this

해설

1, 2, 4, 6, 9, 11, 12, 15 ▸ this와 that은 단수 명사, 단수 동사와 함께 쓴다.

3, 5, 7, 8, 10, 13, 14 ▸ these와 those는 복수 명사, 복수 동사와 함께 쓴다.

B

1 These are new bikes.

2 Those are my cats.

3 These desks are mine.

4 Those letters are for Peter.

5 Are these your umbrellas?

6 Are those your books?

7 I like these pictures.

8 Look at those clouds.

9 Pass me those pencils.

10 These are fun games.

해설

1, 2, 5, 6, 10 ▸ 주어가 복수이면 동사와 보어도 모두 복수여야 한다.

3, 4 ▸ 지시형용사 these/those 뒤에는 복수 명사가 온다. 주어

영작 술술

pp.42~43

A

1 <u>This is</u> today's newspaper.
2 <u>These are</u> Paul's boots.
3 <u>Is that</u> your homeroom teacher?
4 <u>Those are</u> Amy's glasses.
5 Did you write <u>this song</u>?
6 Are <u>those towels</u> wet?
7 No, <u>these are</u> not mine.
8 Look at <u>that flower</u>. It is beautiful.
9 <u>Those people</u> sing badly.
10 We don't need <u>this dictionary</u>.

B

1 This is my favorite perfume.
2 That is the post office.
3 This is my sister Jessica.
4 These blankets are warm.
5 Those shoes are expensive.
6 Are those famous actors?
7 Is this sweater yours?
8 Are these empty boxes?
9 This soup is delicious.
10 That student writes well.

WRAP UP

pp.44~45

A

1 These	2 Those	3 that
4 these	5 That	6 This
7 those		

해설

1 ▸ 동사 are와 보어 my clothes가 복수이므로 주어도 복수(These)여야 한다.
2 ▸ 동사 are와 보어 beautiful earrings가 복수이므로 주어도 복수(Those)가 알맞다.
3 ▸ Is가 단수 동사이므로 주어도 단수(that)여야 한다.
4 ▸ jeans가 복수이므로 these가 알맞다.
5 ▸ cat이 단수이므로 That이 알맞다.
6 ▸ soap이 단수이므로 This가 알맞다.
7 ▸ windows가 복수이므로 those가 알맞다.

B

1 This is my pencil case.
2 That ticket is free.
3 Is this your coat?
4 Those are his socks.
5 These cookies are delicious.

C

1 ④		2 ④	

해설

1 ▸ picture가 단수이므로 those → that
2 ▸ 장미 여러 송이를 의미하므로 these roses가 알맞다.

개념 Review

❶ this	❷ that	❸ 지시형용사
❹ these	❺ those	❻ 복수 명사

ACTUAL TEST

pp.46~47

01 ②	02 ④	03 ①	04 ④
05 ②	06 That, window		
07 ④	08 ③	09 ④	

10 I like Italy. It is a beautiful country.
11 These are not my slippers. They are hers.

12 ③	13 ④

14 This computer is ours.
15 Those students are my classmates.

해설

01 '그것은 내가 좋아하는 계절이다.'라는 의미가 적절하므로 It is가 알맞다.
02 my keys를 대신할 수 있는 말은 mine(나의 것)이다.
03 these는 복수를 의미하므로 단수 명사인 tea는 올 수 없다.
04 '그들은 모두 똑똑하다.'라는 의미가 적절하므로 They are가 알맞다.
05 '그것의 색깔'이 적절하므로 Its가 알맞다.
06 단수 동사 is가 쓰였으므로 Those windows는 That window로 바꿔 써야 한다.
07 동사 took 뒤에는 목적격인 them(그것들)이 와야 한다.
08 '내 자리'는 my seat, '네 자리'는 your seat = yours로 쓸 수 있다.
09 '저 산들'은 Those mountains이고 복수이므로 복수 동사 are를 써야 한다.
10 Italy는 단수이므로 대명사 It으로 받는다. They are → It is
11 '그녀의 것'을 뜻하는 소유대명사는 hers이다.
12 ① Ours car → Our car, ② I → me, ④ He → His로 고쳐야 한다.

13 ① This is → These are 또는 tall trees → a tall tree, ② That → Those, ③ Are these → Is this 또는 rain-coat → raincoats로 고쳐야 한다.

14 '이 컴퓨터'는 This computer, '우리의 것'은 ours이다.

15 '저 학생들'은 Those students, '나의'는 my이다.

Chapter 03 There & It

UNIT 01 There is/are

PRACTICE 1   p.50

1 There is	2 There are
3 There is	4 There are

해설

There is 뒤에는 셀 수 있는 단수 명사나 셀 수 없는 명사가, There are 뒤에는 셀 수 있는 복수 명사가 온다.

PRACTICE 2   p.51

1 Is there a clock on the wall?

2 There isn't an elevator in this building.

3 Are there any dogs in the park?

4 There aren't any pencils in my pencil case.

해설

There is/are 구문의 부정문은 There isn't/aren't ~이고, 의문문은 Is/Are there ~?이다.

문법 쏙쏙   pp.52~53

A

1 is	2 are	3 is
4 are	5 is	6 is
7 are	8 is	9 are
10 are	11 is	12 are
13 is	14 are	15 is

해설

1, 3, 5, 6, 11, 15 ▶ 주어가 단수이면 There is를 사용한다.

2, 4, 7, 9, 10, 12 ▶ 주어가 복수이면 There are를 사용한다.

8, 13 ▶ 주어가 셀 수 없는 명사이면 양에 상관없이 단수 취급하여 There is를 사용한다.

14 ▶ some fish(물고기 몇 마리)는 복수를 의미하므로 There are를 사용한다.

B

1 is	2 Is	3 aren't
4 Is	5 are	6 is
7 isn't	8 Are	9 Is
10 are	11 Are	12 Is
13 aren't	14 is	15 isn't

해설

1, 2, 6, 7, 12, 14, 15 ▶ 주어가 단수이면 be동사는 is를 사용한다.

3, 5, 8, 10, 11, 13 ▶ 주어가 복수이면 be동사는 are를 사용한다.

4, 9 ▶ 주어가 셀 수 없는 명사이면 양에 상관없이 be동사는 is를 사용한다.

영작 술술   pp.54~55

A

1 There is a hole in my sock.

2 There are five children on the playground.

3 There is some tea in the teapot.

4 There isn't a big shopping mall near here.

5 There isn't any water in the bottle.

6 There aren't any eggs in the refrigerator.

7 Is there a train at 8 o'clock?

8 Are there any tickets for the show?

9 Are there many mistakes in my writing?

10 Is there too much butter on your bread?

B

1 There is a gift for you.

2 There is some milk in the glass.

3 There are three bedrooms in the house.

4 There isn't a car in the parking lot.

5 There isn't any sugar in my coffee.

6 There aren't many people in the shop.

7 Is there a swimming pool near here?

8 Are there many flowers in the garden?

9 Is there any food on the table?

10 Are there many mountains in your country?

WRAP UP   pp.56~57

A

1 There is a hair in my soup.

2 There are some people outside.

3 There is a woman at the door.

4 Is there a flight at 7:30?

5 There is a lot of rice in the jar.

6 Are there any problems with it?

7 There aren't any books in the bag.

1 ▶ a hair(머리카락)가 단수이므로 There is를 사용한다.

2 ▶ some people이 복수이므로 There are를 사용한다.

3 ▶ a woman이 단수이므로 There is를 사용한다.

4 ▶ a flight가 단수이므로 Is there를 사용한다.

5 ▶ a lot of는 '많은'의 뜻이지만 rice가 셀 수 없는 명사로 단수 취급하므로 There is를 사용한다.

6 ▶ any problems는 복수이므로 Are there를 사용한다.

7 ▶ any books는 복수이므로 There aren't를 사용한다.

B

1 There is an ant on the paper.

2 There aren't any books on the shelf.

3 Is there a bus to the airport?

4 There is a lot of water on the floor.

5 Are there many parks in your town?

C   **1** ④   **2** ③

해설

1 ▶ people, socks, potatoes는 복수로 There are가 오지만, 셀 수 없는 명사인 snow는 양에 상관 없이 단수 취급하므로 There is가 온다.

2 ▶ '~이 있다'는 There is/are 구문을 사용하고 a car는 단수이므로 There is를 사용한다.

개념 Review

❶ 단수 주어   ❷ 복수 주어   ❸ There is

❹ not   ❺ there

UNIT 02 비인칭 주어 It

PRACTICE 1   p.58

1 It	**2** It
3 There	**4** it

해설

시간, 날짜, 요일이 '~이다'라고 말할 때는 it을 주어로 사용한다. '~이 있다'는 There is/are 구문을 사용한다.

PRACTICE 2   p.59

1 It	**2** There
3 it	**4** It

해설

날씨, 계절, 거리가 '~이다'라고 말할 때도 it을 주어로 사용한다.

문법 쏙쏙   pp.60~61

A

1 It is	**2** There is	**3** It is
4 it is	**5** Is it	**6** It was
7 There is	**8** It was	**9** There was
10 Is it	**11** It is	**12** Is it
13 There is	**14** It is	**15** It is

해설

1, 3, 4, 5, 6, 8, 10, 11, 12, 14, 15 ▶ 시간, 날짜, 요일, 날씨, 계절, 거리에 대해 말할 때는 비인칭 주어 it을 사용한다.

2, 7, 13 ▶ '~이 있다'라고 말할 때는 There is/are 구문을 사용한다.

9 ▶ 날씨에 대해 말하지만 '폭우(heavy rain)가 있었다'는 의미로 명사가 쓰였을 때는 There is/are 구문을 사용한다.

B

1 It	**2** There	**3** it
4 It	**5** there	**6** It
7 it	**8** It	**9** There
10 It	**11** It	**12** It
13 There	**14** It	**15** It

해설

1, 4, 6, 7, 8, 10, 11, 12, 14, 15 ▶ 시간, 날짜, 요일, 날씨, 계절, 거리에 대해 말할 때 비인칭 주어 it을 사용한다.

2, 5, 9 ▶ 어떤 장소에 '~이 있다'라고 말할 때는 There is/are 구문을 사용한다.

3 ▶ '눈이 내리고 있다'는 It is snowing이며 의문문은 Is it snowing?이 된다.

13 ▶ '강풍(a strong wind)이 있다'라고 명사로 날씨를 표현할 때는 There is/are 구문을 사용한다.

영작 술술   pp.62~63

A

1 It is 11:30.

2 It was sunny last weekend.

3 It is not Tuesday today.

4 It is 3 o'clock in the afternoon.

5 It snowed a lot last winter.

6 It is my parents' wedding anniversary.

7 Is it far from here to the airport?

8 Was it your birthday yesterday?

9 It is a 5-minute walk to the post office.

10 It is <u>not</u> very hot today.

③은 '그것'을 의미하는 인칭대명사이다.
2 ▸ 거리를 나타낼 때는 비인칭 주어 it을 사용한다.

B

1 It is June 10.

2 It is only 5 o'clock.

3 It is already fall.

4 It is 1 kilometer from here to the bus stop.

5 Is it Thursday today?

6 It is sunny and warm.

7 Is it November 1 tomorrow?

8 It was Gina's birthday yesterday.

9 It rains in London very often.

10 It is a two-hour drive to the airport.

WRAP UP

A

1 It's time to go home.

2 Is it 7:30 now?

3 It wasn't foggy yesterday.

4 It is a nice day today.

5 It is raining outside.

6 It doesn't snow in Taiwan.

7 It is not Friday today.

해설
1 ▸ Its는 '그것의'라는 의미이므로 It's[It is]로 고쳐야 한다.
2 ▸ 시간에 대해 말할 때는 비인칭 주어 it을 사용한다.
Is this → Is it
3 ▸ 어제의 날씨이므로 isn't → wasn't
4, 5 ▸ 날씨에 대해 말할 때는 비인칭 주어 it을 사용한다.
This is, There is → It is
6 ▸ snow(눈이 오다)는 일반동사이고 날씨에 대해 말하므로 it doesn't를 사용해 부정문을 만든다.
7 ▸ 요일에 대해 말할 때는 비인칭 주어 it을 사용한다.
That is → It is

B

1 It is very cloudy outside.

2 It is already 7 o'clock.

3 It didn't rain yesterday.

4 Is it October 1 today?

5 It is a 30-minute walk to the park.

C   **1** ③   **2** ②

해설
1 ▸ ①, ②, ④는 시간, 날씨, 거리 등을 나타내는 비인칭 주어이나,

개념 Review
❶ 비인칭   ❷ it   ❸ 그것
❹ it

ACTUAL TEST

01 ②	**02** ②	**03** ③	**04** ③
05 ③	**06** There are		
07 ②	**08** ③	**09** ④	

10 Are there any pens in the drawer?

11 It is 5 kilometers from my house to the hospital.

12 ④   **13** ②

14 Are there many people in the mall?

15 It is warm and sunny today.

해설
01 '서점이 있나요?'라는 의미로 a bookstore가 단수이므로 Is there를 사용해 묻는다.
02 '몇 시예요?'라는 질문에 2시라고 답하는 내용으로 비인칭 주어 it을 사용한다.
03 cheese는 셀 수 없는 명사로 단수 취급하므로 There are와 쓸 수 없다.
04 ①, ②, ④는 비인칭 주어이고 ③은 '그것은'이라는 의미의 인칭대명사이다.
05 계절을 말할 때는 비인칭 주어 it을 사용해 나타내고, '~이 있다'는 There is/are 구문을 사용한다. many flowers가 복수이므로 There are가 알맞다.
06 '~이 있다'는 There is/are 구문을 사용하되, 뒤에 three students가 복수이므로 There are를 쓴다.
07 bread는 셀 수 없는 명사로 양에 상관 없이 단수 취급하므로 are를 is로 고쳐야 한다.
08 any peaches는 복수이므로 Is를 Are로 고쳐야 한다.
09 rain은 '비가 오다'라는 의미의 일반동사이므로 isn't 대신 doesn't를 사용해 부정문을 만든다.
10 '~이 있나요?'는 Is/Are there ~?로 나타낸다.
11 거리는 비인칭 주어 it을 사용해 나타낸다.
12 '연필 두 자루와 자 한 개(two pencils and a ruler)'는 복수이므로 There are를 사용한다.
13 '눈이 내리다'는 It snows이고 의문문은 Does it snow? 이다.
14 many people은 복수이므로 Is there를 Are there로 고쳐야 한다.
15 날씨는 비인칭 주어 it을 사용해 나타낸다. There is → It is

10 Grammar Plus Writing Start 2

UNIT 01 형용사의 쓰임

PRACTICE 1   p.70

1 cold	2 difficult
3 dirty	4 old

해설
형용사는 명사 앞에서 뒤에 오는 명사를 꾸며준다.

PRACTICE 2   p.71

1 big	2 fast
3 salty	4 beautiful

해설
형용사는 be동사나 감각동사 feel/look/taste/smell/sound 뒤에 쓰여 주어의 상태를 나타낸다.

문법 쏙쏙   pp.72~73

A

1	famous	2	old
3	fresh	4	hot
5	delicious	6	thick
7	bitter	8	colorful
9	ugly	10	dangerous
11	big	12	long
13	wonderful	14	new, comfortable
15	warm, soft		

해설
1, 2, 4, 6, 8, 10, 12, 13, 14 ▸ 형용사는 명사 앞에서 뒤에 오는 명사를 꾸며준다.
3, 5, 7, 9, 11, 14, 15 ▸ 형용사는 be동사나 감각동사 뒤에 쓰여 주어의 상태를 나타낸다.

B

1 This is an (✔) book.
2 Robert is happy with his (✔) job.
3 She writes (✔) songs.
4 Jane looks (✔) today.
5 Mr. Brown is (✔) to people.
6 Linda brushed her (✔) hair.
7 Turtles are (✔) runners.
8 The students felt (✔) after the exam.
9 My uncle has a very (✔) dog.
10 Susan bought a (✔) table.
11 Your idea sounds (✔).
12 Science class is (✔) for me.
13 Tomatoes are a (✔) food.
14 Nurses help (✔) people.
15 She put the money in a (✔) place.

해설
1, 2, 3, 6, 7, 9, 10, 13, 14, 15 ▸ 형용사는 명사 앞에서 뒤에 오는 명사를 꾸며준다. 이때 「관사/소유격＋형용사＋명사」의 어순에 주의한다.
4, 5, 8, 11, 12 ▸ 형용사는 be동사나 감각동사 뒤에 쓰여 주어의 상태를 나타낸다.

영작 술술   pp.74~75

A

1 It was a big mistake.
2 The giraffe has a long neck.
3 She is wearing a blue coat.
4 The ladder is safe.
5 The plan sounds interesting.
6 The pillow is soft and comfortable.
7 The backpack looks heavy.
8 His jokes are always funny.
9 The steak doesn't taste good.
10 The children felt scared.

B

1 He is a kind person.
2 Baseball is a popular sport.
3 You look lovely today.
4 It was a boring movie.
5 This room is small and dirty.
6 The young businessman is rich.
7 We felt bored.
8 He lived in two different countries.
9 The dark chocolate tastes bitter.
10 The car engine sounds smooth.

WRAP UP   pp.76~77

A

1 This watch is too expensive.

2 He has a white cat.

3 Beth looks sad today.

4 That is an interesting idea.

5 Bob sold his old car.

6 The tower is very tall.

7 My mom's soup tastes great.

해설

1▸ expensive는 '비싼'이며, '비싸다'는 「be동사(is)+expensive」로 나타낸다.

2▸ 「관사+형용사+명사」의 어순이므로 a white cat으로 쓴다.

3▸ 「look+형용사」는 '~해 보이다'의 의미이다.

4▸ 「관사+형용사+명사」의 어순이므로 an interesting idea로 쓴다.

5▸ 「소유격+형용사+명사」의 어순이므로 his old car로 쓴다.

6▸ tall은 '높은'이며, '높다'는 「be동사(is)+tall」로 나타낸다.

7▸ 「taste+형용사」는 '맛이 ~하다'의 의미이다.

B

1 The glass is empty.

2 We don't have enough money.

3 Your English is very good.

4 The old couple looks happy.

5 The festival was boring.

C **1** ③   **2** ③

해설

1▸ '~해 보이다'는 「look+형용사」이므로 danger(위험) → dangerous(위험한)가 알맞다.

2▸ 「관사+형용사+명사」의 어순이므로 The new English teacher이고, '친절하다'는 「be동사(is)+kind」이다. very는 kind를 강조하는 말로 kind 앞에 온다.

개념 Review

❶ 앞   ❷ be동사   ❸ 감각

❹ 상태

UNIT 02 수량형용사

PRACTICE 1   p.78

1 Did you buy much food?

2 I ate many apples.

3 He doesn't have much money.

4 Did you take many pictures?

해설

many 뒤에는 셀 수 있는 명사의 복수형, much 뒤에는 셀 수 없는 명사가 온다.

PRACTICE 2   p.79

1 some		**2** any	
3 some		**4** any	

해설

some은 긍정문에 any는 부정문과 의문문에 사용한다.

문법 쏙쏙   pp.80~81

A

1 many	**2** much	**3** a lot of
4 a lot of	**5** much	**6** a lot of
7 a lot of	**8** Many	**9** a lot of
10 many	**11** much	**12** a lot of
13 many	**14** a lot of	**15** many

해설

셀 수 있는 명사의 복수 앞에는 many, a lot of, 셀 수 없는 명사 앞에는 much, a lot of를 사용한다.

B

1 some	**2** OK	**3** any
4 some	**5** any	**6** some
7 OK	**8** OK	**9** some
10 OK	**11** any	**12** OK
13 some	**14** any	**15** OK

해설

some은 긍정문에 any는 부정문과 의문문에 사용한다.

영작 술술   pp.82~83

A

1 I watched some movies.

2 He drinks a lot of water.

3 There are many people on the street.

4 They have too much work to do.

5 I sent her some flowers.

6 He doesn't have any friends.

7 There isn't much milk at home.

8 Did you buy any butter yesterday?

9 Mary got many cards on her birthday.

10 He spends a lot of time in front of the TV.

B

1 Do you save much[a lot of] money?
2 We bought a lot of food.
3 I read some books every month.
4 Do you eat many[a lot of] vegetables?
5 Do you have any brothers or sisters?
6 There are many[a lot of] people on the bus.
7 She buys many[a lot of] clothes.
8 I need some help.
9 Sandra doesn't have any free time.
10 Is there much[a lot of] cheese on the dish?

WRAP UP

pp.84~85

A

1 Some students passed the test.
2 I read many[a lot of] books on vacation.
3 We got some snow last winter.
4 He has too much work to do.
5 Are there any gifts for me?
6 Some people went to the zoo.
7 He put a lot of salt in the soup.

해설

1▸ some 뒤에는 셀 수 있는 명사의 복수형이 온다.
2▸ 셀 수 있는 명사 앞에는 many, a lot of를 사용한다.
3▸ 긍정문에서는 some을 사용한다.
4▸ 셀 수 없는 명사 앞에 '너무 많은'은 too much를 사용한다.
5▸ any 뒤에 셀 수 있는 명사는 복수형이 온다.
6▸ 긍정문에서는 some을 사용한다.
7▸ 긍정문에서 셀 수 없는 명사 앞에 '많은'은 a lot of를 사용한다.

B

1 My little brother has many[a lot of] toys.
2 We didn't buy much[a lot of] chocolate.
3 Many[A lot of] students were sick.
4 There is some sugar in the juice.
5 She doesn't need any advice.

C 1 ④   2 ②

해설

1▸ ① much → many[a lot of], ② any → some, ③ many → a lot of가 알맞다.
2▸ 부정문에서는 any를 써야 하며, luck은 셀 수 없는 명사로 a를 붙이거나 복수형을 만들 수 없다.

개념 Review

❶ many ❷ much ❸ a lot of
❹ some ❺ any

ACTUAL TEST

pp.86~87

01 ③   02 ④   03 ②   04 ②
05 ①
06 Basketball players are tall.
07 This tea smells good.
08 ④   09 ③   10 ①   11 ④
12 ①   13 ③
14 I usually have a big breakfast.
15 We saw some lions at the zoo.

해설

01 명사 dancer를 꾸며주는 형용사 good(훌륭한)이 알맞다.
02 셀 수 없는 명사 milk와 어울리면서 부정문에 쓸 수 있는 것은 much이다.
03 부정문에서는 some 대신 any를 쓴다.
04 형용사 앞에 be동사와 감각동사가 올 수 있다. 동사 has 뒤에는 명사를 취해야 한다.
05 food는 셀 수 없는 명사이므로 many와 쓸 수 없다.
06 '키가 크다'는 「be동사+tall」로 나타낸다.
07 '~한 향[냄새]이 나다'는 「smell+형용사」로 나타낸다.
08 felt tired는 '피곤을 느꼈다'이다.
09 '많은'을 의미하고 셀 수 있는 명사 movies와 쓸 수 있는 말은 many이다.
10 「a/an+형용사+명사」의 어순이므로 a yellow bag으로 고쳐야 한다.
11 부정문이므로 some을 any로 고쳐야 한다.
12 「소유격+형용사+명사」의 어순이므로 His new bike이고, '~해 보이다'는 「look+형용사」로 나타낸다.
13 부정문에서 셀 수 없는 명사 sunshine 앞에는 any, much가 사용 가능하나 의미상 much가 알맞다.
14 「a/an+형용사+명사」의 어순이므로 a big breakfast가 되어야 한다.
15 some 뒤에 셀 수 있는 명사는 복수형이 온다. lion → lions

Chapter 05 부사

PRACTICE 1
p.90

1 brightly	2 very
3 Luckily	4 slowly

해설

부사는 동사, 형용사, 다른 부사, 또는 문장 전체를 꾸며주는 역할을 한다.

PRACTICE 2
p.91

1 kindly	2 easily
3 seriously	4 angrily
5 greatly	6 strangely
7 fast	8 well

해설

대부분의 부사는 형용사에 -ly를 붙여 만들며, 「자음+y」로 끝나는 형용사는 y를 i로 고치고 -ly를 붙인다. fast, late, high, hard, early는 형용사와 부사의 형태가 같고, good의 부사형은 well이다.

문법 쏙쏙
pp.92~93

A

1 hard	2 safe	3 badly
4 early	5 fast	6 late
7 Suddenly	8 easily	9 strange
10 beautifully	11 carefully	12 angry
13 heavily	14 high	15 serious

해설

1 ▶ 동사 works를 수식하므로 부사가 와야 하며, hard는 형용사와 부사의 형태가 같다.
2 ▶ 명사 city를 수식하므로 형용사인 safe가 온다.
3 ▶ 동사 hurt를 수식하므로 부사인 badly가 온다.
4 ▶ 동사 woke up을 수식하므로 부사가 와야 하며, early는 형용사와 부사의 형태가 같다.
5 ▶ 동사 runs를 수식하므로 부사가 와야 하며, fast는 형용사와 부사의 형태가 같다.
6 ▶ be동사 뒤에는 보어로 형용사가 오며, late는 형용사와 부사의 형태가 같다.
7 ▶ 문장 전체를 수식하는 부사인 Suddenly가 와야 한다.
8 ▶ 동사 solved를 수식하므로 부사인 easily가 온다.
9 ▶ 명사 dream을 수식하므로 형용사인 strange가 온다.

10 ▶ 동사 dances를 수식하므로 부사인 beautifully가 온다.
11 ▶ 동사 carried를 수식하므로 부사인 carefully가 온다.
12 ▶ 동사 looked 뒤에는 보어로 형용사인 angry가 온다.
13 ▶ 동사 rained를 수식하므로 부사인 heavily가 온다.
14 ▶ 동사 jumped를 수식하므로 부사가 와야 하며, high는 형용사와 부사의 형태가 같다.
15 ▶ 명사 problem을 수식하므로 형용사인 serious가 온다.

B

1 quickly	2 loudly	3 carefully
4 politely	5 easily	6 fast
7 Strangely	8 nicely	9 high
10 Surprisingly	11 hard	12 early
13 well	14 angrily	15 late

해설

1, 2, 3, 4, 7, 8, 10 ▶ 대부분의 부사는 형용사에 -ly를 붙여 만든다.
5, 14 ▶ 「자음+y」로 끝나는 형용사는 y를 i로 고치고 -ly를 붙인다.
6, 9, 11, 12, 15 ▶ fast, high, hard, early, late는 형용사와 부사의 형태가 같다.
13 ▶ 형용사 good의 부사형은 well이다.

영작 술술
pp.94~95

A

1 He opened the door quietly.
2 She dressed beautifully.
3 Jack plays the guitar very well.
4 She tasted the tea carefully.
5 Aaron walks too fast.
6 Tom answered the question easily.
7 The children crossed the street safely.
8 She looked at me sadly.
9 I returned the books late.
10 They played together happily.

B

1 I broke the egg carefully.
2 She left the party early.
3 Luckily, he found his watch.
4 The bus arrived late.
5 The student raised his hand high.
6 The train stopped suddenly.
7 Minsu speaks English well.
8 Ruth drives her car fast.
9 Jessica came into the classroom quietly.
10 My grandmother walked slowly.

WRAP UP

A

1 Jack ate his lunch quickly.
2 The dog barks loudly.
3 Paul is a nice man.
4 Mike ran to school fast.
5 The apple pie smells delicious.
6 We all studied hard.
7 James cooks very well.

해설

1 > 동사 ate를 수식하므로 부사인 quickly가 알맞다.
2 > 동사 barks를 수식하므로 부사인 loudly가 알맞다.
3 > 명사 man을 수식하므로 형용사인 nice가 알맞다.
4 > fast는 형용사와 부사의 형태가 같다.
5 > '~한 냄새가 나다'는 「smell+형용사」이다. deliciously →
delicious
6 > '열심히'를 뜻하는 부사는 hard이다.
7 > '요리를 매우 잘 한다'의 의미이므로 good의 부사형 well이
알맞다.

B

1 Peter dances very well.
2 He read the book loudly.
3 She opened the present slowly.
4 Our team played badly.
5 They ate their dinner late.

C   1 ②   2 ②

해설

1 > hard는 형용사와 부사의 형태가 같다. hardly는 또 다른 부
사로 '거의 ~ 않다'를 의미한다.
2 > be동사의 보어로 쓰였으므로 형용사인 kind를 써야 한다.

개념 Review

❶ 앞/뒤   ❷ 앞   ❸ 앞/뒤
❹ -ly   ❺ i   ❻ -ly

UNIT 02 빈도부사

PRACTICE 1

1 always   2 usually
3 often   4 never

해설

빈도부사는 횟수를 나타내는 부사로, always(항상), usually(보
통, 대개), often(자주, 종종), sometimes(가끔, 때때로), rare-
ly(거의 ~않다), never(결코 ~않다) 등이 있다.

PRACTICE 2

1 The man (✓) tells lies.
2 They are (✓) busy on Monday.
3 My sister (✓) eats after 7:00 p.m.
4 Do you (✓) help your mother?

해설

빈도부사는 일반동사 앞, be동사나 조동사 뒤에 위치한다. 의문
문에서는 주어 뒤에 온다.

문법 쏙쏙

A

1 Jack (✓) has lunch at a restaurant.
2 Eric (✓) fights with his friends.
3 Our classroom is (✓) clean.
4 Mrs. Lee is (✓) nice to her students.
5 We (✓) go shopping on Saturday afternoon.
6 Do you (✓) feel sad?
7 My dog (✓) barks at people.
8 I will (✓) visit you in New York.
9 He (✓) goes to the pool in the morning.
10 I am (✓) nervous before interviews.
11 I will (✓) forget your kindness.
12 Is the school bus (✓) on time?
13 Laura (✓) has ice cream for dessert.
14 Kate and James are (✓) cheerful.
15 Peter (✓) leaves his cellphone on the table.

해설

1, 2, 5, 7, 9, 13, 15 > 긍정문에서 빈도부사는 일반동사 앞에 위치
한다.
3, 4, 10, 14 > 긍정문에서 빈도부사는 be동사 뒤에 위치한다.
6, 12 > 의문문에서 빈도부사는 주어 뒤에 위치한다.
8, 11 > 긍정문에서 빈도부사는 조동사(will) 뒤에 위치한다.

B

1 I usually take a shower in the morning.
2 Does he often surf the Internet?
3 Mike is always a good student.
4 I usually go to bed at midnight.
5 She never eats fast food.
6 Is the park usually crowded?
7 She sometimes takes a nap in the afternoon.

8 I usually do the laundry on Saturday.

9 I will always remember you.

10 Tom rarely gets up early.

해설

1, 4, 5, 7, 8, 10 > 긍정문에서 빈도부사는 일반동사 앞에 위치한다.

2, 6 > 의문문에서 빈도부사는 주어 뒤에 위치한다.

3 > 긍정문에서 빈도부사는 be동사 뒤에 위치한다.

9 > 긍정문에서 빈도부사는 조동사(will) 뒤에 위치한다.

영작 술술

pp.102~103

A

1 She usually plays the piano in her free time.

2 I am always happy to see you.

3 It often snows here in the winter.

4 He rarely cleans his room.

5 She never sings or dances.

6 Bob is usually free after school.

7 Do you sometimes listen to the radio?

8 I will never be late again.

9 Is it always hot in Africa?

10 I usually go for a walk after dinner.

B

1 Our math teacher rarely smiles.

2 I often lose my umbrella.

3 I rarely understand his English.

4 His advice is always helpful.

5 Tony usually goes to school by bike.

6 Do you always wear glasses?

7 I will never see you again.

8 Kelly usually skips dinner.

9 Do you sometimes go camping?

10 She is rarely late for school.

WRAP UP

pp.104~105

A

1 I always do my homework.

2 Mary is usually friendly.

3 He is rarely at the library.

4 I will never tell a lie.

5 Harry sometimes wears a suit.

6 John often goes to the gym.

7 Do you always see her?

해설

1, 5, 6 > 긍정문에서 빈도부사는 일반동사 앞에 위치한다.

2 > 긍정문에서 빈도부사는 be동사 뒤에 위치한다.

3, 4 > 빈도부사 rarely(거의 ~않다)와 never(결코 ~않다)는 not과 함께 쓸 수 없다.

7 > 의문문에서 빈도부사는 주어 뒤에 위치한다.

B

1 He sometimes goes to the movies.

2 I will never forget his name.

3 She always wears sunglasses in summer.

4 George often plays soccer after school.

5 Lily is rarely late for class.

C　　**1** ②　　　　　　**2** ①

해설

1 > 빈도부사는 be동사 뒤에 위치한다.

2 > go는 일반동사이므로 rarely는 go 앞에 온다.

개념 Review

❶ 횟수　　　　❷ not　　　　❸ 앞
❹ 뒤　　　　　❺ 주어

ACTUAL TEST

pp.106~107

01 ①	02 ④	03 ④	04 ③
05 ④	06 easily	07 high	
08 ②	09 ①	10 ④	11 ①
12 ②	13 ①		

14 Josh usually goes to school by bus.

15 Is he often late for work?

해설

01 '열심히'를 뜻하는 부사는 hard이다. ② hardly는 '거의 ~ 않다'라는 의미이다.

02 주어가 3인칭 단수이므로 동사는 drives이고, 빈도부사 always는 일반동사 drives 앞에 온다.

03 fast는 형용사와 부사의 형태가 같다.

04 ③ early는 명사 breakfast를 꾸며주는 형용사로 쓰였고, 나머지는 부사이다.

05 ④ '늦게'를 뜻하는 부사는 late이다.

06 '쉽게'는 형용사 easy(쉬운)의 부사형 easily이다.

07 high는 형용사와 부사의 형태가 같다.

08 '~하게 보이다'는 「look+형용사」이다. ② lovely(예쁜)는 -ly로 끝나지만 형용사이다.

09 '빨리'를 뜻하는 부사는 fast이고, fastly로 쓰지 않는다.

10 high는 형용사와 부사의 형태가 같다. highly → high

11 빈도부사는 be동사 뒤에 위치한다. never is → is never

12 명사 actor를 수식하는 것은 형용사이므로 great, 동사 acts를 수식하는 것은 부사이므로 well을 쓴다.

13 빈도부사는 일반동사 앞에 위치하고, rarely(거의 ~않다)는 부정어 not과 함께 쓸 수 없다.

14 빈도부사 usually는 일반동사 goes 앞에 위치한다.

15 의문문에서 빈도부사는 주어 뒤에 위치한다.

Chapter 06 의문사

UNIT 01 When, Where, Why

PRACTICE 1 p.110

1 Where		**2** When	
3 Why		**4** Where	

해설

의문사 when은 때, where는 장소, why는 이유를 물을 때 사용한다.

PRACTICE 2 p.111

1 is		**2** were	
3 did		**4** does	

해설

be동사가 있는 문장의 의문사 의문문은 「의문사＋be동사＋주어 ~?」의 형태이고, 일반동사가 있는 문장의 의문사 의문문은 「의문사＋do/does/did＋주어＋동사원형 ~?」의 형태이다.

문법 쏙쏙 pp.112~113

A

1 When		**2** Where		**3** Why	
4 When		**5** When		**6** Where	
7 Where		**8** Why		**9** When	
10 Where		**11** Where		**12** When	
13 When		**14** Why		**15** Where	

해설

1, 4, 5, 9, 12, 13 ▷ 때에 대해 물을 때는 의문사 when을 사용한다.

2, 6, 7, 10, 11, 15 ▷ 장소에 대해 물을 때는 의문사 where를 사용한다.

3, 8, 14 ▷ 이유에 대해 물을 때는 의문사 why를 사용한다.

B

1 When is Jack's birthday party?

2 Where is your school?

3 Why is Peggy sad?

4 When do you get up every morning?

5 Where does he come from?

6 Where are they going?

7 When did you visit your grandparents?

8 Why did you go to the dentist?

9 Where did they go yesterday?

10 Why did the driver stop?

해설

1, 4, 7 ▷ 때에 대해 물을 때는 의문사 when을 사용한다.

2, 5, 6, 9 ▷ 장소에 대해 물을 때는 의문사 where를 사용한다.

3, 8, 10 ▷ 이유에 대해 물을 때는 의문사 why를 사용한다.

영작 술술 pp.114~115

A

1 <u>Where</u> <u>is</u> the post office?

2 <u>When</u> <u>is</u> her wedding?

3 <u>Why</u> <u>are</u> <u>they</u> excited?

4 <u>When</u> <u>were</u> <u>you</u> born?

5 <u>Why</u> <u>is</u> she <u>wearing</u> sunglasses?

6 <u>Where</u> <u>does</u> your father <u>work</u>?

7 <u>When</u> <u>did</u> the train <u>arrive</u>?

8 <u>Why</u> <u>did</u> you <u>call</u> me last night?

9 <u>Where</u> <u>did</u> you <u>go</u> for your vacation?

10 <u>When</u> <u>did</u> you <u>buy</u> that new book?

B

1 Where is your cellphone?

2 When is the math test?

3 Why is the girl crying?

4 Where are the children playing?

5 Why was Jenny late yesterday?

6 When did you finish your homework?

7 Where did you grow up?

8 Why did she go to the airport yesterday?

9 Where did you buy that dress?

10 When did you send the email?

WRAP UP

pp.116~117

A

1 Where is City Hall?

2 When did you meet him?

3 When is your birthday?

4 Where did they go?

5 Why are you so happy?

6 Where is he?

7 Why did you buy that book?

> **해설**
>
> **1, 5** ▸ be동사의 의문사 의문문은 「의문사+be동사+주어 ~?」의 어순이다.
>
> **2** ▸ 일반동사 과거 의문문은 did를 사용한다. you met → did you meet
>
> **3** ▸ 때에 대해 물을 때는 의문사 when을 사용한다.
>
> **4** ▸ 일반동사의 의문사 의문문은 「의문사+do/does/did+주어+동사원형 ~?」의 형태이다.
>
> **6** ▸ 이 문장에서 '그'는 주어에 해당하므로 him → he
>
> **7** ▸ 일반동사 과거 의문문은 did를 사용한다. you bought → did you buy

B

1 Where is the drugstore?

2 When do the banks open?

3 Where did you find it?

4 When did you start working here?

5 Why did he meet Julie?

C 1 ② 2 ②

> **해설**
>
> **1** ▸ be동사의 의문사 의문문은 「의문사+be동사+주어 ~?」의 어순이다. Why she is always busy? → Why is she ~?
>
> **2** ▸ 일반동사(meet)가 쓰인 의문문이므로 조동사 do를 넣어 만들되, 과거 시제이므로 did를 사용한다.

> **개념 Review**
>
> ❶ when ❷ where ❸ why
> ❹ Yes/No ❺ be동사 ❻ 일반동사

UNIT 02 Who, What

PRACTICE 1

p.118

1 Who   2 What

3 What   4 Who

> **해설**
>
> '누구'라고 물을 때는 who, '무엇'이라고 물을 때는 what을 사용한다.

PRACTICE 2

p.119

1 Who   2 What

3 Who   4 What

> **해설**
>
> '누구'라고 물을 때는 who, '무엇'이라고 물을 때는 what을 사용한다.

문법 쏙쏙

pp.120~121

A

1 Who	2 What	3 Who
4 What	5 Who	6 What
7 Who	8 What	9 Who
10 What	11 Who	12 What
13 Who	14 What	15 Who

> **해설**
>
> **1, 3, 5, 7, 9, 11, 13, 15** ▸ '누구(누가, 누구를)'라는 의미는 의문사 who를 사용한다.
>
> **2, 6, 8, 10, 14** ▸ '무엇(무엇이, 무엇을)'이라는 의미는 의문사 what을 사용한다.
>
> **4, 12** ▸ '무슨 색', '무슨 운동'이므로 의문사 what이 알맞다.

B

1 What is your brother's name?

2 Who designed the house?

3 Who did Jack see at the park?

4 What are the boys playing?

5 Who invited Nick to dinner?

6 Who did you visit last weekend?

7 What did you have for lunch?

8 What fell off the ceiling?

9 What did she drop?

10 Who is grading the tests?

> **해설**
>
> **1, 3, 4, 6, 7, 9** ▸ 의문사가 목적어나 보어를 대신할 경우 be동사가 있으면 「의문사+be동사+주어 ~?」, 일반동사가 있으면 「의문사+do/does/did+주어+동사원형 ~?」 형태이다.
>
> **2, 5, 8, 10** ▸ 의문사 who나 what이 주어로 쓰이면 바로 뒤에 동사가 와서 「의문사+동사 ~?」의 어순이 된다.

영작 술술

pp.122~123

A

1 <u>Who is</u> your favorite teacher?
2 <u>What is</u> in your bag?
3 <u>Who moved</u> the boxes?
4 <u>What is he reading</u>?
5 <u>What happened</u> to you?
6 <u>Who do</u> you want to talk to?
7 <u>Who did</u> you <u>meet</u> yesterday?
8 <u>Who is going to</u> do the dishes?
9 <u>What movie did</u> you watch yesterday?
10 <u>What did</u> you <u>buy</u> last weekend?

B

1 Who is that girl?
2 What is your favorite TV show?
3 What is in the drawer?
4 Who cleaned this room?
5 Who does Sam like?
6 What do you usually do on the weekend?
7 What is she cooking?
8 What did you ask during class?
9 Who did you invite to dinner?
10 What book are you reading?

WRAP UP

pp.124~125

A

1 Who is Andrew?
2 What are you doing?
3 What is his address?
4 Who won the prize?
5 What did you do last weekend?
6 Who made this pasta?
7 What happened last night?

해설

1, 2 ▸ be동사의 의문사 의문문은 「의문사+be동사+주어 ~?」의 어순이다.
3 ▸ '그의 주소는 무엇이니?'라고 해야 하므로 의문사 Who를 What으로 고쳐야 한다.
4, 6, 7 ▸ 의문사 who나 what이 주어로 쓰이면 조동사 do를 쓰지 않고 의문사 뒤에 바로 동사가 온다.
5 ▸ '무엇을 했나요?'는 What did you do ~?가 되어야 한다.

B

1 Who are they?
2 What is your favorite food?
3 What game did you play?
4 Who failed the exam?
5 What do you usually do after school?

C 1 ②   2 ①

해설

1 ▸ ② '누가 그 사고를 보았습니까?'라는 의미이므로 의문사 who을 써서 묻는다.
2 ▸ who가 주어로 쓰이므로 의문사 뒤에 바로 동사 opened가 온다.

개념 Review

❶ who   ❷ what   ❸ 명사
❹ 주어

UNIT 03 How

PRACTICE 1

p.126

1 He's good.
2 It was terrible.
3 They played very well.
4 I walked.

해설

의문사 how는 '어떤, 어떻게'라는 의미로, 주로 상태, 방법, 수단 등을 물을 때 사용한다.

PRACTICE 2

p.127

1 tall   2 big
3 well   4 often

해설

how tall은 키나 높이, how big은 크기, how well은 '얼마나 잘', how often은 횟수나 빈도를 물을 때 쓴다.

문법 쏙쏙

pp.128~129

A

1 How are you today?
2 How is the coffee?
3 How is the weather in Alaska?

4 How does Jane dance?

5 How does she look in that dress?

6 How do Jack and Peggy go to school?

7 How tall is the basketball player?

8 How old is the temple?

9 How long did you study last night?

10 How often does your mom do grocery shopping?

해설

1, 2, 3, 4, 5, 6 ▶ '어떤, 어떻게'라고 상태, 방법, 수단 등을 물을 때 how를 사용한다.

7 ▶ 키, 높이는 how tall로 묻는다.

8 ▶ '얼마나 오래된'은 how old로 묻는다.

9 ▶ 기간, 길이는 how long으로 묻는다.

10 ▶ 횟수, 빈도는 how often으로 묻는다.

B

1 How are you feeling today?

2 How was your trip to Japan?

3 How did Carol sing?

4 How did they solve the problem?

5 How does Mary go to work?

6 How did you travel in Europe?

7 How big is the new shopping mall?

8 How old is your brother?

9 How far is the hospital from here?

10 How often do you have P.E. class?

해설

1, 2 ▶ be동사의 의문사 의문문은 「의문사＋be동사＋주어 ～?」의 어순이다.

3, 4, 5, 6 ▶ 일반동사의 의문사 의문문은 「의문사＋do동사＋주어 ＋일반동사 ～?」의 어순이다.

7, 8, 9, 10 ▶ 의문사 how는 「how＋형용사/부사」 형태로 쓰여 다양한 의미를 갖는다.

영작 술술

pp.130~131

A

1 How are your parents?

2 How was your trip to Thailand?

3 How do I look in this dress?

4 How does he go to work?

5 How did you find the watch?

6 How far is the station from here?

7 How tall is your father?

8 How long did he stay in New York?

9 How often does it snow in Korea?

10 How well did she sing?

B

1 How is the weather today?

2 How was your summer vacation?

3 How does Michael go to school?

4 How did you first meet your boyfriend?

5 How big is the pond?

6 How old is Gyeongbok Palace?

7 How far is the gas station from here?

8 How often do you eat out?

9 How well did they play?

10 How long did he live in Canada?

WRAP UP

pp.132~133

A

1 How was	**2** How does
3 How did	**4** How does
5 How tall	**6** How far
7 How often	

해설

1 ▶ '공연은 어땠습니까?'라는 의미로 be동사 was가 필요하다.

2 ▶ 일반동사 drive가 쓰였고 주어가 he이므로 does를 써서 의문문을 만든다.

3 ▶ 일반동사 make가 쓰였고 과거의 일이므로 did를 써서 의문문을 만든다.

4 ▶ 일반동사 go가 쓰였고 주어가 he이므로 does를 써서 의문문을 만든다.

5 ▶ 키를 물을 때는 how tall로 묻는다.

6 ▶ 거리를 물을 때는 how far로 묻는다.

7 ▶ 횟수, 빈도를 물을 때는 how often으로 묻는다.

B

1 How was the movie?

2 How do I get to City Hall?

3 How big is your dog?

4 How well does he work?

5 How often do you get a haircut?

C　　**1** ③　　　　　　　**2** ④

해설

1 ▶ ①, ②, ④는 how가 가능하지만, ③은 what으로 물어야 한다.

2 ▶ 횟수는 how often으로 묻는다. 일반동사가 쓰였으므로 「의문사＋do/does/did＋주어＋동사원형 ～?」의 어순이 된다.

ACTUAL TEST

pp.134~135

01 ③	**02** ②	**03** ③	**04** ④
05 ②	**06** Who	**07** How far	
08 ③	**09** ③	**10** Where	
11 What	**12** ②	**13** ①	

14 What subject do you like

15 How often does he drive to work

해설

01 '일요일에.'라고 대답했으므로 '때'를 묻는 의문사 when이 알맞다.

02 '수수께끼를 풀고 있어.'라고 대답했으므로 그들이 '무엇을' 하는지를 묻고 있는 의문사 what이 알맞다.

03 '내가 샀어.'라고 대답했으므로 '누가' 샀는지를 묻는 의문사 who가 알맞다.

04 첫 번째 문장은 Who, Where, How가 모두 가능하지만, 두 번째 문장은 How만 가능하다.

05 교통 수단을 묻는 질문이므로 ②가 알맞다.

06 파티에서 Jack과 Sandy를 만났다고 했으므로 '누구를' 만났는지 물어야 자연스럽다.

07 거리를 묻고 있으므로 How far가 알맞다.

08 once a month(한 달에 한 번)는 횟수를 나타내는 말로, how often으로 물어야 가능한 대답이다.

09 키, 높이는 how tall로 묻는다. how long은 길이나 기간을 물을 때 사용한다.

10 '너는 지난 휴가 때 어디를 갔니?'라는 의미가 자연스러우므로 What을 Where로 고쳐야 한다.

11 '무슨 색으로 문을 칠 할거야?'라는 의미가 돼야 하므로 How color를 What color로 고쳐야 한다.

12 '그 상점에 언제/왜/어떻게 갔습니까?'는 자연스럽지만 Who(누가, 누구를)는 어색하다.

13 의문사 who가 주어로 쓰이면 뒤에 바로 동사 ate가 나와야 한다.

14 '너는 무슨 과목을 좋아하니?'라는 의미가 되도록 What subject ~?로 묻는다.

15 '그는 얼마나 자주 운전해서 직장에 가나요?'라는 의미가 되도록 횟수, 빈도를 묻는 how often을 사용한다.

WORKBOOK ANSWERS

UNIT 01 셀 수 있는 명사
pp.2~3

A

1	O	2	countries
3	mice	4	legs
5	O	6	an umbrella
7	fish	8	tomatoes
9	men	10	O
11	child	12	O
13	sheep	14	O
15	O		

B

1 The beaches have soft sand.
2 My sister loves pink dresses.
3 My family visited an island this summer.
4 Brush your teeth before bed.
5 My neighbors are kind and nice.
6 The baby's feet are so small and cute.
7 Mike broke a few dishes.
8 Leaves change colors in fall.
9 Cities have many people and buildings.
10 Kate put the clothes in the boxes.

UNIT 02 셀 수 없는 명사
pp.4~5

A

1	milk	2	furniture
3	a slice of	4	meat
5	luck	6	bars
7	flowers	8	a bowl of
9	beauty	10	advice
11	loaves	12	water
13	salt	14	time
15	a piece of		

B

1 Italy is famous for food.
2 My friend gave me a box of candy.
3 Saturday is my favorite day.
4 The pudding has a lot of sugar.
5 Ted drank a bottle of mango juice.
6 She saved some money for new shoes.
7 I ate a bar of chocolate for dessert.
8 Do you like to listen to dance music?
9 He was tired from hard work.
10 The waiter brought two glasses of water.

UNIT 01 인칭대명사
pp.6~7

A

1	They	2	Mine	3	her
4	his	5	ours	6	them
7	your	8	I	9	its
10	Yours	11	him	12	Our
13	us	14	his	15	theirs

B

1 I don't remember her face.
2 Are the glasses hers?
3 Will you go swimming with him?
4 Erin helped me with my project.
5 The cute rabbits are his.
6 Is yours on the desk?
7 The family likes to walk their dog.
8 Everyone likes his idea.
9 We played soccer with them.
10 Our teacher reads us interesting stories.

UNIT 02 지시대명사
pp.8~9

A

1	This	2	that
3	these	4	this
5	birds	6	This
7	that	8	these

9 Those   10 these

11 Those are   12 That

13 those   14 this

15 These

B

1 Are these your socks?

2 This is my cousin Sam.

3 That is a famous tower.

4 I borrowed this book from Jake.

5 She made these beautiful paintings.

6 My dad climbs that mountain.

7 Pour that oil into the pan.

8 Those musicians played music together.

9 Are these your family photos?

10 Those are my sister's dresses.

Chapter 03 There & It

UNIT 01 There is / are   pp.10~11

A

1 is   2 are

3 isn't   4 Are

5 aren't   6 are

7 Is   8 isn't

9 are   10 Is

11 aren't   12 is

13 are   14 Are

15 aren't

B

1 There are some monkeys in the tree.

2 There is a big lake in the city.

3 There are many cafés along the street.

4 Is there a bank near here?

5 There aren't[are not] many stars in the sky.

6 There isn't[is not] any soap in the bathroom.

7 There are 12 months in a year.

8 There is a lot of bread on the shelf.

9 Are there soccer players on the field?

10 There aren't[are not] many new buildings in Rome.

UNIT 02 비인칭 주어 It   pp.12~13

A

1 it   2 It

3 there   4 It

5 It   6 It

7 There   8 it

9 it   10 it

11 There   12 It

13 It   14 It

15 There

B

1 It was hot and sunny today.

2 Is it 9 o'clock in New York now?

3 It was a busy weekend.

4 It is going to be windy tomorrow.

5 Is it Sue's birthday today?

6 It is not far from my house to the park.

7 It is summer in Sydney now.

8 Was it June 1 yesterday?

9 It is raining a lot here.

10 It is a 30-minute drive to the office.

Chapter 04 형용사

UNIT 01 형용사의 쓰임   pp.14~15

A

1 His car is (✓) and broken.

2 We had a (✓) weekend.

3 Lemons taste too (✓).

4 The movie is not (✓).

5 She is a (✓) singer in Korea.

6 The fog is (✓) today.

7 Her baby looks lovely and (✓).

8 Emily felt (✓) after the hard work.

9 I bought a (✓) T-shirt online.

10 The flowers smell (✓).

11 Daniel has (✓) hair.

12 My grandmother made me (✓) cookies.

13 Don't do that. It's (✓).

14 There is a (✓) house near here.

15 It is (✔) in winter in Alaska.

B

1 The old house looks scary.
2 Fresh vegetables are healthy.
3 Josh is a clever student.
4 Your idea sounds great.
5 We had a wonderful dinner.
6 The traffic is heavy today.
7 I feel comfortable at home.
8 There is a long bridge over there.
9 The roller coaster is very fast.
10 Mr. Brown has colorful neckties.

_{UNIT} **02 수량형용사**   pp.16~17

A

1 many[a lot of]		**2** O	
3 O		**4** much[a lot of]	
5 many[a lot of]		**6** O	
7 much[a lot of]		**8** books	
9 O		**10** some	
11 O		**12** much[a lot of]	
13 any		**14** O	
15 many[a lot of]			

B

1 There are many tourists in Paris.
2 We got a lot of rain this summer.
3 There isn't any bread on the plate.
4 I saw some beautiful clouds in the sky.
5 Do you have any questions?
6 A lot of children enjoy playing games.
7 I need some fruit and eggs.
8 My neighbor makes a lot of noise.
9 We didn't catch many fish.
10 Anny didn't do much homework.

Chapter 05 부사

_{UNIT} **01 부사의 쓰임**   pp.18~19

A

1 kind		**2** carefully	
3 so fast		**4** easily	
5 Luckily		**6** beautifully	
7 well		**8** healthy	
9 suddenly		**10** hard	
11 Strangely		**12** sad	
13 quietly		**14** early	
15 seriously			

B

1 He drank the tea slowly.
2 The children laughed loudly.
3 He threw the ball high.
4 Plants don't grow well in the desert.
5 She left the party quickly.
6 We think differently about it.
7 She danced so beautifully on the stage.
8 Josh shouted angrily at his brother.
9 We studied very hard for the test.
10 Erin said hello to her neighbor nicely.

_{UNIT} **02 빈도부사**   pp.20~21

A

1 often go fishing		**2** never eats	
3 O		**4** sometimes have	
5 rarely play		**6** is always	
7 O		**8** O	
9 is rarely		**10** he often late	
11 am sometimes		**12** O	
13 is often curious		**14** usually have	
15 O			

B

1 They rarely climb the mountain.
2 She is always kind to her friends.
3 I usually walk my dog after dinner.
4 My family sometimes goes camping on Saturday.
5 The mall is often crowded with people.

6 Do you usually go to bed late?

7 I will never visit the restaurant again.

8 Are you sometimes sleepy after lunch?

9 We rarely see stars in the city.

10 He always takes the subway to work.

Chapter 06 의문사

UNIT 01 When, Where, Why
pp.22~23

A

1	When	**2**	Why
3	Where	**4**	When
5	Why	**6**	Where
7	When	**8**	Where
9	Why	**10**	When
11	Where	**12**	Why
13	When	**14**	Where
15	Why		

B

1 Where did you lose your bag?

2 Why are you feeling happy today?

3 When did you visit Canada?

4 Why was he angry at you?

5 Where does your brother work?

6 When did you get the present?

7 Where were you born?

8 When do you go jogging?

9 Why does Charles look so tired?

10 When does summer vacation start?

UNIT 02 Who, What
pp.24~25

A

1	Who	**2**	What
3	What	**4**	Who
5	What	**6**	Who
7	What	**8**	Who
9	What	**10**	Who
11	What	**12**	What
13	What	**14**	Who
15	Who		

B

1 What is on the sofa?

2 Who solved the quiz?

3 Who did you call last night?

4 What are the children making there?

5 Who sent you the nice gift?

6 What do you usually eat for breakfast?

7 What is your dream job?

8 Who is singing the song loudly?

9 Who do you like to play with?

10 What did you see at the zoo?

UNIT 03 How
pp.26~27

A

1	How was	**2**	How did
3	How well	**4**	How often
5	How far	**6**	How long
7	How did	**8**	How tall
9	How old	**10**	How big
11	How long	**12**	How was
13	How often	**14**	How old
15	How do		

B

1 How big is the shopping mall?

2 How far is the post office from here?

3 How are you feeling today?

4 How often does your family eat out?

5 How old is the bridge over there?

6 How well did he do on the test?

7 How tall is your little brother?

8 How did you find this nice restaurant?

9 How long did it take to get there?

10 How did they finish the homework quickly?